AFTER THE SIXTH SEAL

THE RESURRECTION OF OVERCOMERS

PAUL BORTOLAZZO

AFTER THE SIXTH SEAL

ISBN-
ISBN-
Available in Hardcover, Paperback, eBook.

Prophecy Charts: Francis Hernandez

Published by Hemingway Publishers
Cover design by Hemingway Publishers
ISBN: Printed in the United States

“But the Helper, the Holy Spirit, whom the Father will send in My name, He will teach you all things, and bring to your remembrance all things that I said to you.” JOHN 14:26

TABLE OF CONTENT

Resurrection of Overcomers

Day of The Lord

Prophecy Charts

This Page Intentionally Left Blank

1

The Sign of Your Coming

'Now as He sat on the Mount of Olives, the disciples came to Him privately, saying, "Tell us, when will these things be? And what will be the sign of Your coming, and of the end of the age?" Matthew 24:3

The afternoon crowd heard every word. His pronouncement of His people was harsh. Because of their rebellion, their temple will be destroyed. Turning away from the courtyard, Jesus crossed over the Kidron Valley up to the Mount of Olives. Peter, James, John and Andrew followed Him. **(Mark 13:3)** The tension that night was like no other. His death for the sins of the world was just days away. In this late hour, His disciples could have asked many questions. Their urgency was about His promise to return. **(John 14:1-4)** They wanted to know the sign of His Second Coming. **(Mat. 24:3)** Jesus taught them much more. **(Mat. 24:33)**

"Watch therefore, and pray always that you may be counted worthy to escape all these things that will come to pass, and to stand before the Son of Man." Luke 21:36

During His ministry on earth, Jesus taught His followers the Coming of The Son of Man. **(Luke 12:40)** A time when believers will be rewarded according to their works. **(Mat. 16:27)** Just days before His death, our Lord shared a new revelation. Jesus taught a series of events taking place before His Coming. **(Mat. 24:3-33)** His exhortation to watch and not be deceived was chilling. How so? Only those escaping these events will stand before the Son of Man! **(Luke 21:36)**

"... 'When it is evening you say, 'It will be fair weather, for the sky is red' and in the morning, 'It will be foul weather today, for the sky is red and threatening.' Hypocrites. You know how to discern the face of the sky, but you cannot discern the signs of the times." Matthew 16:2-3

During His First Coming, Jesus was upset with those claiming to understand the signs of the times. It didn't matter how many Old Testament scriptures He cited. The miracles He did could not change their minds. Even the lives transformed by the power of God meant nothing to them. **(John 21:25)** These hypocrites were not able to discern the signs of His First Coming. **(Mat. 16:2-3)** Today, history is repeating itself. Most Christians are not discerning the signs of His Second Coming. **(Isa. 13:9-11, Mat. 16:27)** The sign of the Day of The Lord followed by the sign of The Son of Man on the same day! **(Mat. 24:29-30)**

"But he who endures to the end shall be saved." Matthew 10:22

In this late hour, a divine urgency is spreading through the body of Christ. Yet, most are not understanding its meaning! The answer is simple yet profound. The Spirit of God is preparing a great multitude to physically endure till the harvest! Why is this necessary? Tragically, many ministers are no longer making disciples capable of overcoming. On a typical Sunday morning, you will hear these popular deceptions taking away from The Revelation of Jesus Christ:
"The resurrection of believers can happen at any moment!"
(False)
"The church won't be here for the Antichrist!"
(False)
"You can suffer in the Great Tribulation; I'll be in heaven!"
(False)
"It doesn't matter when Jesus gathers us, let's just be ready!"
(False)

"...When the Son of Man comes, will He really find faith on the earth?" Luke 18:8

Why will there be such a lack of faith when the Son of Man comes back? **(Luke 18:8)** It's because Jesus will return during a time of trouble never seen before. **(Mat. 24:21-22)** A time when the world will hate anyone proclaiming His Name! A time when the wicked will prosper, while believers suffer. **(Mat. 24:9-13)** Then why are most Christians refusing to believe this? **(Luke 21:8)** It's due to widespread apostasy. So many having a form of godliness are denying the power of God! **(2 Tim. 3:1-5)** To be clear, Jesus is coming back for a faithful bride. **(Rev. 7:9-17)**

"But, Paul, how can we know when Jesus will come back? No one can know for sure! Tell me, why should I study ***AFTER THE SIXTH SEAL?"***

'He who overcomes shall be clothed in white garments, and I will not blot out his name from the Book of Life; but I will confess his name before My Father and before His angels.' Revelation 3:5

Jesus has told us when to look up for our redemption. **(Luke 21:25-28)** After the Lamb opens the **Sixth Seal**, the sun, moon, and stars will lose their light. **(Mat. 24:29, Rev. 6:12-17)** Trapped in darkness, every eye will see the Son coming back in the glory of His Father. **(Rev. 1:7, Mat. 16:27)** On this day, a great multitude of overcomers will not be blotted out of the Book of Life! **(Rev. 7:9-17)** Instead, the Son will confess their names before His Father! **(Rev. 3:5)**

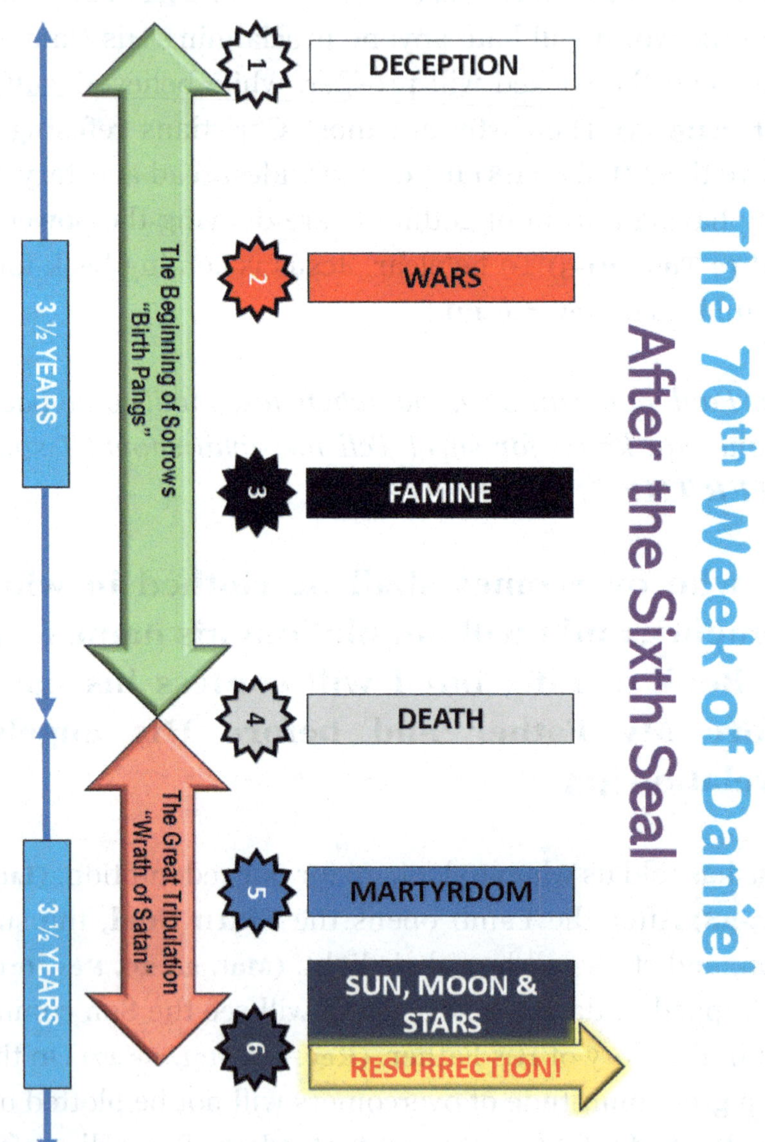
The 70th Week of Daniel
After the Sixth Seal
1
DECEPTION
2
WARS
3
FAMINE
4
DEATH
5
MARTYRDOM
6
SUN, MOON & STARS
RESURRECTION!
The Beginning of Sorrows
"Birth Pangs"
The Great Tribulation
"Wrath of Satan"
3 ½ YEARS
3 ½ YEARS

2

The Days of Noah

"And as it was in the days of Noah, so it will be also in the days of the Son of Man." Luke 17:26

While on the Mount of Olives (33 A.D.), Jesus taught the most complete description of the Coming of The Son of Man. **(Mat. 24:3-44)** An event initiating His Second Coming. After His death on the cross, Peter, James, John and Andrew went forth sharing what Jesus taught them that night. **(Mark 13:3)** In the 60's, God chose four disciples to write their gospels. Matthew, Mark, and Luke each wrote down an account of Christ's Olivet Discourse. **(Matthew 24-25, Mark 13, Luke 21)** Even though he was there that night, John didn't write about it in his gospel. Instead, Jesus chose him to witness in a vision, the events taking place before, during, and after His Second Coming. The apostle wrote down what he saw in 96 A.D. His letter is called, The Revelation of Jesus Christ! **(Rev. 1:1)**

"I am He who lives, and was dead, and behold, I am alive forevermore. Amen. And I have the keys of Hades and of Death. Write the things which you have seen, and the things which are, and the things which will take place after this." Revelation 1:18-19

Throughout history, the most respected theologians, scholars, and pastors have taught the Second Coming is a single event. Even though John described four visits Jesus will fulfill during His future Second Coming.

The *Coming* of The **SON of MAN**! **(Rev. 7:9-17)**
The *Return* of The **HOLY ONE**! **(Rev. 10:1-7)**
The *Appearing* of The **WORD OF GOD**! **(Rev. 19:11-21)**
The *Arrival* of The **LAMB OF GOD! (Rev. 21:9-10)**

'But each one in his own order: Christ the firstfruits, afterward those who are Christ's at His coming.' 1 Corinthians 15:23

Let's say I taught a prophecy seminar last week in Orlando. I arrived on Friday and taught an evening session. The next day I taught a morning session. That afternoon I taped a radio show. Before returning home, I preached two services on Sunday. My coming to Florida included everything I did while I was there. The same can be said for the events Jesus will accomplish during His Second Coming.

‘Remember therefore how you have received and heard; hold fast and repent. Therefore if you will not watch, I will come upon you as a thief, and you will not know what hour I will come upon you.’ Revelation 3:5

In his vision, John saw four visits by Jesus. During His Second Coming, they will take place at different times, for different reasons, each having a different result. **(Rev. 7:9-17; 10:1-7; 19:11-21; 21:9-10)** Is this true? Let’s find out by comparing the Coming of The Son of Man with the appearing of The Word of God.

“But as the days of Noah were, so also will the coming of the Son of Man be. For as in the days before the flood, they were eating and drinking, marrying, and giving in marriage, until the day that Noah entered the ark, and did not know until the flood came and took them all away, so also will the coming of the Son of Man be.” Matthew 24:37-39

In Noah’s day, the wicked were eating, drinking, and getting married. **(Mat. 24:37-39)** Until God closed the door to the ark! **(Gen. 7:13-17)** The wicked were unaware of their destruction until it started to rain! So how will the coming of the Son of Man be like the days of Noah? **(Luke 17:30)** The same day the righteous are taken to heaven, God’s wrath will punish the wicked left behind! **(Mat. 24:40-42)**

"But on the day that Lot went out of Sodom it rained fire and brimstone from heaven and destroyed them all. Even so will it be in the day when the Son of Man is revealed." Luke 17:29-30

Jesus also compared His Coming to the days of Lot. **(Luke 17:29-30)** The same day he left Sodom; fire came down and destroyed the wicked. Which means the same day the Son of Man is revealed, fire will begin destroying sinners. **(Rev. 8:1-7)**

"...It will come as destruction from the Almighty...Behold, the day of the Lord comes, Cruel, with both wrath and fierce anger, to lay the land desolate; And He will destroy its sinners from it...I will punish the world for its evil, And the wicked for their iniquity..." Isaiah 13:6, 9, 11

During the Day of The Lord, the world will be punished for its evil, the wicked for their iniquity. **(Isa. 13:6-11)** This destruction is from the Almighty! His wrath will destroy sinners while laying the land desolate! And when will the great and awesome Day of The Lord erupt? These Old Testament prophets tell us. **(Isa. 13:9-11, Joel 2:31, Zep. 1:14, Ezek. 32:7, Obad. 1:15, Amos 5:18)**

"The sun shall be turned into darkness, And the moon into blood, Before the coming of the great and awesome day of the LORD." Joel 2:31

After the opening of the **Sixth Seal** on the outside of the heavenly scroll, the constellations will lose their light. **(Rev. 5:1; 6:12-17)** This is the sign of the Day of The Lord. **(Isa. 13:9-11, Joel 2:31, Mat. 24:29)** Cloaked in darkness, every eye will see the Son coming back in the glory of His Father with His angels. **(Mat. 16:27)** This is the sign of The Son of Man. **(Mat. 24:27, 30)**

'Now I saw heaven opened, and behold, a white horse. And He who sat on him was called Faithful and True, and in righteousness He judges and makes war. His eyes were like a flame of fire, and on His head were many crowns. He had a name written that no one knew except Himself. He was clothed with a robe dipped in blood, and His name is called The Word of God.' Revelation 19:11-13

In his vision, John saw the Word of God riding on a white horse at the supper of the great God. **(Rev. 19:11-13)** Jesus is coming back to judge the wicked and make war. He is clothed with a robe dipped in blood. His eyes are like fire. On His head are many crowns. Out of His mouth is a sword to strike the nations with. **(Rev. 19:21)** Armies of angels clothed in fine linen are with Him. **(Rev. 15:6; 19:14)**

'Then the beast was captured, and with him the false prophet who worked signs in his presence, by which he deceived those who received the mark of the beast and those who worshiped his image. These

two were cast alive into the lake of fire burning with brimstone.' Revelation 19:20

The Word of God will begin by casting the Beast and his False Prophet into the lake of fire. **(Rev. 19:20)** And when will the birds eat dead flesh at the supper of the Great God? This same day Jesus will kill every follower of the Beast! **(Rev. 19:21)** This will happen after the pouring out of the **Seventh Bowl**. **(Rev. 16:17-21)** At this point, one third of mankind is dead. The cities have fallen. The oceans, rivers, and lakes are infected. Those having the mark of the Beast will be gnawing in pain from their sores. **(Rev. 16:1-2)** Clearly, the wicked won't be eating, drinking, and having fun on the eve of Armageddon. **(Luke 17:26-30, Rev. 16:14-16)**

"But the day of the Lord will come as a thief in the night, in which the heavens will pass away with a great noise, and the elements will melt with fervent heat; both the earth and the works that are in it will be burned up." 2 Peter 3:10

So how will Jesus fulfill these two events during His Second Coming? The Day of The Lord will come back as a thief in the night to an unsuspecting world. **(2 Pet. 3:10)** The Son of Man will take believers to heaven before melting the earth with fervent heat. I emphasize again **(Luke 17:26-30)**, Jesus will deliver His elect before pouring out His wrath on the wicked left behind. **(Rev. 7:9-17; 8:2; 16:1-21)**

'Then I saw another sign in heaven, great and marvelous: seven angels having the seven last plagues, for in them the wrath of God is complete.' Revelation 15:1

The Day of The Lord will end when the last seven plagues are completed. **(Rev. 15:1; 16:1-21)** Once the **Seventh Bowl** is poured out on the wicked **(Rev. 16:17)**, the Word will appear at the supper of the great God. **(Rev. 19:11-21)** Which proves the Coming of the Son of Man and the appearing of the Word of God will take place at different times, for different reasons, each having a different result. Clearly, His Second Coming will have a beginning and an ending. **(Rev. 7:9-17; 21:9-10)**

'Paul, Silvanus, and Timothy, to the church of the Thessalonians in God the Father and the Lord Jesus Christ: Grace to you and peace from God our Father and the Lord Jesus Christ.' 1 Thessalonians 1:1

The year was 49 A.D. The apostle Paul was imprisoned for sharing the gospel of Jesus Christ. His future looked hopeless. Suddenly, from within his jail cell, a miracle took place. While he was praying the Spirit of God led him to write a letter. It was addressed to the church in Thessalonica. **(1 Thes. 1:1)** The main subject is the Coming of our Lord Jesus Christ. **(1 Thes. 3:13, 4:15-17)** The same coming Jesus taught while on the Mount of Olives. **(Mat. 24:30-31, Mark 13:24-27, Luke 21:25-28)** This is why Paul concluded each chapter with a reference to the Second Coming! **(1 Thes. 1:10, 2:19, 3:13, 4:15, 5:23)**

'And to wait for His Son from heaven, whom He raised from the dead, even Jesus who delivers us from the wrath to come.' 1 Thessalonians 1:10

(1) Everyone waiting for the Son will be delivered before the Day of The Lord erupts worldwide! **(1 Thes. 1:10)** A great multitude of overcomers will be caught up to the throne of God before the wicked are destroyed. **(Rev. 7:9-17, Isa. 13:9-11)** This is the fulfillment of His promise to come again. **(John 14:1-4)**

'For what is our hope, or joy, or crown of rejoicing? Is it not even you in the presence of our Lord Jesus Christ at His coming?' 1 Thessalonians 2:19

(2) Paul was rejoicing! His future hope is to see his brothers and sisters in Christ. **(1 Thes. 2:19)** To experience the joy of being in the presence of our Lord Jesus Christ at His Coming! **(Titus 2:11-13)** It will be a glorious time when believers are rewarded for their works by the Son of Man. **(Mat. 16:27; 24:29-31)**

'So that He may establish your hearts blameless in holiness before our God and Father at the coming of our Lord Jesus Christ with all His saints.'
1 Thessalonians 3:13

(3) At this moment, the dead in Christ are with the Lord! **(2 Cor. 5:8)** Their decaying bodies are in the graves! At the coming of our Lord Jesus Christ, His saints from heaven will be with Him. **(1 Thes. 3:13)** They're looking forward to their glorious resurrection with alive believers on earth! **(1 Thes. 4:13-17; Mark 13:26-27)**

'Then we who are alive and remain shall be caught up together with them in the clouds to meet the Lord in the air. And thus we shall always be with the Lord.' 1 Thessalonians 4:17

(4) The overcomers surviving the Great Tribulation will be caught up in the clouds with believers from heaven. **(Mark 13:24-27, Rev. 7:9-17)** In the twinkling of an eye, they will meet their Lord in the air. **(1 Cor. 15:50-52, 1 Thes. 4:15-17)**

'Now may the God of peace Himself sanctify you completely; and may your whole spirit, soul, and body be preserved blameless at the coming of our Lord Jesus Christ.' 1 Thessalonians 5:23

(5) We can feel Paul's love for his brethren. He prayed for the God of peace to completely sanctify them. To preserve them at the coming of our Lord Jesus Christ. **(1 Thes. 5:23)** If someone can't depart from their faith, then why was Paul praying for believers to be found blameless at His Coming? Why was he stressing the perseverance of the saints? The first century believers needed this powerful encouragement.

So will those during the future Great Tribulation. **(Rev. 7:9-17)**

'Now, brethren, concerning the coming of our Lord Jesus Christ and our being gathered to him, we ask you.' 2 Thessalonians 2:1

So, is the gathering of believers taught by Paul, the same gathering taught by Jesus? **(1 Thes. 4:13-17, Mark 13:24-27)** In both accounts, Jesus is coming in the clouds. **(1 Thes. 4:17, Mat. 24:30)** He is coming like a thief! **(1 Thes. 5:4, Luke 12:39)** A trumpet will sound! **(1 Thes. 4:16, Mat. 24:31)** Dead and alive believers are caught up! **(1 Thes. 4:16-17, Mark 13:26-27)** Jesus and Paul are describing the resurrection of believers at His Coming! Yet, none of the above events will take place at the battle of Armageddon. **(Rev. 16:14-16; 19:11-21)**

"For this we say to you by the word of the Lord, that we who are alive and remain until the coming of the Lord will by no means precede those who are asleep." 1 Thessalonians 4:15

Then what does Paul mean '*by the word of the Lord*'? After His death on the cross, Peter, James, John, and Andrew shared the events Jesus taught them while on the Mount of Olives. **(Mark 13:3)** In his letter, Paul is repeating their description of the Coming of The Son of Man! **(Matthew 24:30, Mark 13:26, Luke 21:27)** He calls this resurrection of believers, the Coming of The Lord! **(1 Thes. 4:15)**

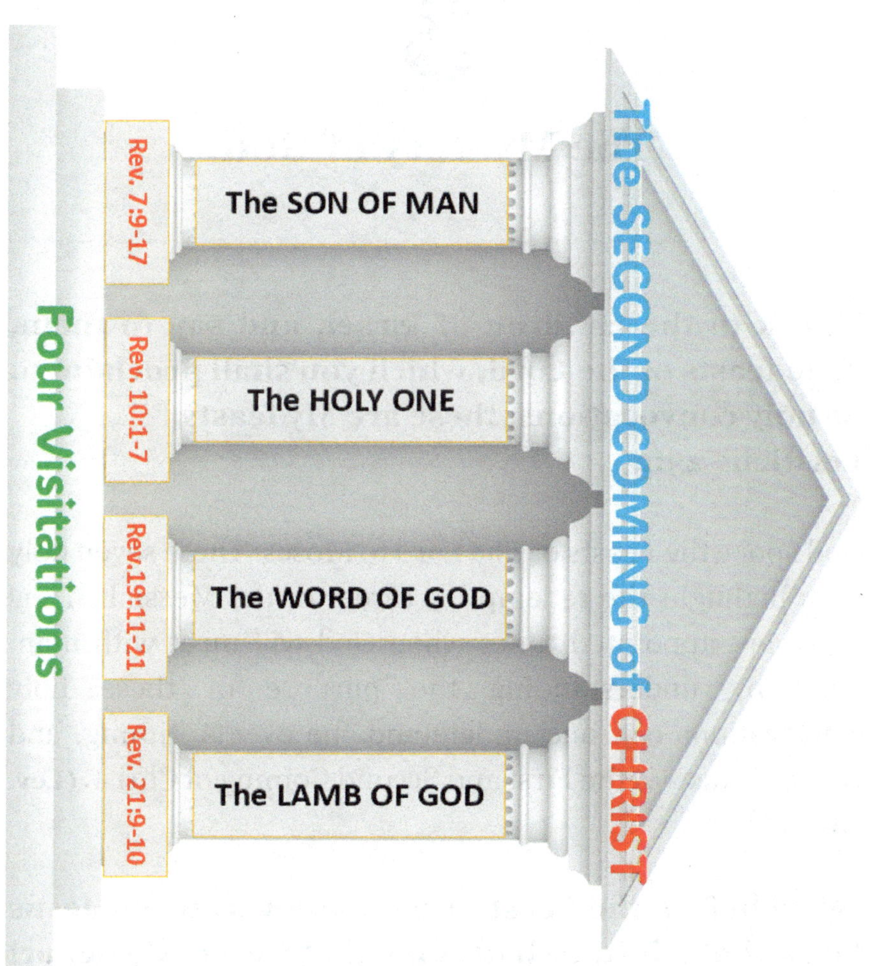
The SECOND COMING of CHRIST
The SON OF MAN
Rev. 7:9-17
The HOLY ONE
Rev. 10:1-7
The WORD OF GOD
Rev.19:11-21
The LAMB OF GOD
Rev. 21:9-10
Four Visitations

3

The Mystery of God

'Speak to the children of Israel, and say to them, "The feasts of the Lord, which you shall proclaim to be holy convocations, these are My feasts."
Leviticus 23:2

God spoke the Feasts of The Lord to Moses. These seven holy days highlight the redemptive career of the Messiah. They represent appointed times when God will meet with man. Only by understanding the purpose of these holy convocations can one understand the events, timing, and consequences of the First and Second Coming of Christ. **(Lev. 23:1-44)**

"Now before the Feast of the Passover, when Jesus knew that His hour had come that He should depart from this world to the Father, having loved His own who were in the world, He loved them to the end."
John 13:1

During His First Coming, our Messiah fulfilled the first four Feasts of The Lord. **(Lev. 24:4)** The Feast of Passover represents His shedding of blood on the cross for the sins of the world. **(Isa. 53:4-6, 1 Pet. 1:19, 1 John 2:1-2)** The Feast of Unleavened Bread represents the time His body did not decay in the grave. **(Psa. 16:10, Acts 2:31)** The Feast of First Fruits represents His resurrection from the dead on the third day. **(1 Cor. 15:4, Luke 24:7)** The Feast of Weeks (Pentecost) represents the day believers received the Promise of the Father. **(Acts 1:4-5; 2:1-4)**

'So, Christ was offered once to bear the sins of many. To those who eagerly wait for Him He will appear a second time, apart from sin, for salvation.' Hebrews 9:28

Jesus will fulfill the last three Feasts during His Second Coming.
During the **Feast of Trumpets**, the Son of Man will deliver the righteous before pouring out His wrath on the followers of the Beast. **(Mat. 24:30-39, Rev. 7:9-17)**
During the **Day of Atonement**, the Holy One will spiritually save a remnant from Israel. **(Dan. 9:24, Rom. 11:26-30, Heb. 9:28, Rev. 10:1-7)**

During the **Feast of Tabernacles**, the Lamb of God will harvest all believers before destroying the kingdom of the Beast. **(Rev. 14:1-4, 14-16)**

'The mystery which has been hidden from ages and from generations, but now has been revealed to His saints.' Colossians 1:26

What is a mystery? A biblical mystery is a truth that is beyond human understanding. It can only be understood by the Spirit. In the first century, the Spirit of God revealed three mysteries to the apostle Paul.

(1) The mystery of the church.
(Eph. 3:1-6)
(2) The mystery of the resurrection of alive believers.
(1 Cor. 15:50-52)
(3) The mystery of God, the salvation of Israel.
(Rom. 11:25-27)

'For this reason, I, Paul, the prisoner of Christ Jesus for you Gentiles...how that by revelation He made known to me the mystery...which in other ages was not made known to the sons of men, as it has now been revealed by the Spirit to His holy apostles and prophets: that the Gentiles should be fellow heirs, of the same body, and partakers of His promise in Christ through the gospel.' Ephesians 3:1, 3-6

(1) Paul was a prisoner for preaching Jesus to the Gentiles. From his jail cell, the Holy Spirit revealed a mysterious revelation. A mystery never made known to the sons of men. Gentiles were partaking in the promise in Christ through the gospel. By believing in the death, burial, and resurrection of

Jesus, they are now fellow heirs with believing Jews. Paul taught the Ephesians there is no longer any distinction between Jews and Gentiles. Simply, all believing in Christ are now partakers of the same body! **(Eph. 3:1, 3-6)**

"Behold, I tell you a mystery: We shall not all sleep, but we shall all be changed— in a moment, in the twinkling of an eye, at the last trumpet."
1 Corinthians 15:51

(2) Paul wrote another letter to the believers living in Corinth. The ultimate hope for the dead in Christ is to rise on the last day. **(John 6:44)** Yet, Paul was now teaching a new mystery. **(1 Cor. 15:50-52)** Clearly, a corrupted fleshly body cannot inherit the kingdom of heaven. At the last trump, believers from heaven and earth will be changed, receiving incorruptible bodies. **(1 Cor. 15:35-52)** Then angels will gather them to Jesus. **(2 Thes. 2:1)** This is the resurrection of dead and alive believers at the Coming of The Son of Man. **(1 Thes. 4:15-17, Mark 13:26-27)**

'For I do not desire, brethren, that you should be ignorant of this mystery...that blindness in part has happened to Israel until the fullness of the Gentiles has come in. And so all Israel will be saved...'
Romans 11:25-26

(3) The third mystery given to Paul concerns the future salvation of Israel. The angel Gabriel revealed this prophecy to Daniel. **(Dan. 9:24-27)** Jesus quoted it. **(Mat. 24:1-2, 15, Luke 21:20)** John saw it happen in his vision. **(Rev. 10:1-7)** Paul explained this mystery in a letter to the believers living in Rome. **(Rom. 11:25-27)** He clearly warned believing Gentiles not to be ignorant concerning the future salvation of the Jewish people. The Gentiles grafted into the body of Christ, were boasting about their salvation. Paul reminded them of God's plan of salvation for all. It is true, many Jews were cut off because of their unbelief. **(Rom. 11:17-21)** Why did this have to happen? Although rarely taught, God has committed the Jewish people to disobedience so the Gentiles could be saved. **(Rom. 11:32)** Yet, there is coming a day when their blindness to the gospel will be removed. The Father has promised to give them a new heart and a new spirit. **(Ezek. 36:23-27)** The Jews believing in Jesus during His Second Coming will be saved. **(Heb. 9:28)**

'But in the days of the sounding of the seventh angel, when he is about to sound, the mystery of God would be finished, as He declared to His servants the prophets.' Revelation 10:7

Paul taught Jesus was offered once to bear the sins of many. He also foretold when the Christ will appear a second time. **(Heb. 9:28)** The Most Holy will physically return on the Day of Atonement to fulfill the mystery of God **(Rev. 10:7)**, the salvation of Israel. **(Dan. 9:24)** This will be the first time the Son appears on earth since He left to be with His Father. **(Acts 1:9-11, Rom. 11:25-27)**

"To the Lord our God belong mercy and forgiveness, though we have rebelled against Him. We have not obeyed the voice of the Lord our God, to walk in His laws, which He set before us by His servants the prophets. Yes, all Israel has transgressed Your law, and has departed so as not to obey Your voice; therefore, the curse and the oath written in the Law of Moses the servant of God have been poured out on us, because we have sinned against Him.'
Daniel 9:9-11

The year was 538 B.C.. The children of Israel were transgressing the law. Many were refusing to obey the voice of God. Such rebellion was inviting divine judgment. The prophet understood the consequences. In this dark hour, he was pleading with God to turn away His anger from Jerusalem. Daniel was confessing his sins and the sins of his people when an angel arrived. **(Daniel 9:11-21)**

'..."O Daniel, I have now come forth to give you skill to understand. At the beginning of your supplications the command went out, and I have come to tell you, for you are greatly beloved; therefore consider the matter, and understand the vision." Daniel 9:22-23

Daniel was greatly loved! God heard his prayers for His people. At the beginning of his supplications, the command went out. Gabriel was sent with a vision concerning the future salvation of Israel. This angel gave Daniel the skill to understand this revelation. A truth rarely taught today. **(Dan. 9:22-23)**

"Seventy weeks are determined for your people and for your holy city, To finish the transgression, To make an end of sins, To make reconciliation for iniquity, To bring in everlasting righteousness, To seal up vision and prophecy, and to anoint the Most Holy.' Daniel 9:24

Due to their defiant rebellion, God decreed a chastisement upon the Jewish people. They will be disciplined for seventy weeks. **(Dan. 9:24)** One week represents seven years. For 490 years (70x7=490), the children of Israel will be dominated by her enemies. This prophecy began after Nehemiah was given the command to restore the gates of the temple and the wall of Jerusalem. **(Neh. 2:5-8)** Let's review the five events involving the future salvation of the Jewish people.

"Know therefore and understand, that from the going forth of the command to restore and build Jerusalem Until Messiah the Prince, there shall be seven weeks and sixty-two weeks...And after the sixty-two weeks Messiah shall be cut off, but not for Himself." Daniel 9:25-26

(1) The first event was about the cross. Gabriel told Daniel there will be 69 weeks (483 years) from the order to restore the

walls of Jerusalem until the death of the Messiah. **(Dan. 9:25-26)** This is exactly what happened. The angel predicted the very day the Messiah was cut off. After 483 years, Jesus was crucified for the sins of the world. **(Mark 15:25-34)** The **69th Week** of this prophecy is over. Some Jews were expecting the Most Holy to physically return seven years later. It never happened. In fact, the fulfillment of the **70th Week** (seven years) is still future. **(Dan. 9:24)** Sadly, most pastors don't believe in a gap between the **69th** and **70th Week**. Instead, they're teaching this prophecy was fulfilled in the first century. Why is this not possible? It's because the Most Holy physically returning for the salvation of Israel is still future. Be assured, our Jesus will fulfill the Day of Atonement during His Second Coming. **(Dan. 9:24, Rom. 11:25-27, Heb. 9:28, Rev. 10:1-7)**

'... And the people of the prince who is to come shall destroy the city and the sanctuary.' Daniel 9:26

'Then Jesus went out and departed from the temple, and His disciples came up to show Him the buildings of the temple. And Jesus said to them, "Do you not see all these things? Assuredly, I say to you, not one stone shall be left here upon another, that shall not be thrown down." Matthew 24:1-2

(2) The second event was the destruction of the holy city and the sanctuary. **(Dan. 9:26)** In 70 A.D., Titus led his Roman armies into Jerusalem and killed over one million Jews!

Their temple was destroyed. Jesus correctly prophesied not one stone would be left upon another. **(Mat. 24:1-2)** The result, God scattered the children of Israel throughout the earth. This judgment is called the Great Diaspora. **(Lev. 26:33, Deut. 28:64-65, Dan. 9:26, Luke 19:43-44, Neh. 1:8)**

"Then he shall confirm a covenant with many for one week..." Daniel 9:27

(3) The third event will initiate the future **70th Week** of Daniel. **(Dan. 9:24-27)** The Beast (Little Horn) will confirm a seven-year covenant of peace between the leaders of ten Arab nations (horns) and Israel. **(Dan. 9:27, Rev. 17:11-12, Dan. 7:7-8)** During the first half of the **70th Week** (also called the Beginning of Sorrows), the world will be suffering from wars and rumors of wars. At the same time, the Jewish people will be living in peace! **(Mat. 24:4-8, Rev. 6:1-6)**

"Therefore when you see the 'abomination of desolation,' spoken of by Daniel the prophet, standing in the holy place" (whoever reads, let him understand)." Matthew 24:15

(4) The fourth event will take place in the middle of the **70th Week**. The Beast and his armies will invade an unsuspecting Jerusalem. **(Luke 21:20)** The Abomination of Desolation will stand in the holy place. **(Mat. 24:15)** The Man of Sin will then defile the temple of God. **(2 Thes. 2:3-4)** This sacrilege will initiate the Great Tribulation. At this moment, the cry to

rebuild the temple is at an all-time high. Jesus, Daniel, Paul, and John each mention this future temple. **(Mat. 24:15, Dan. 9:27, 2 Thes. 2:4, Rev. 11:2)** It may be similar in size to the tabernacle Israel used in the wilderness. **(Deut. 8:2, Exod. 28:43)**

'But in the days of the sounding of the seventh angel, when he is about to sound, the mystery of God would be finished, as He declared to His servants the prophets.' Revelation 10:7

(5) The fifth event is the physical return of the Christ at the end of the **70th Week. (Dan. 9:24, Heb. 9:28)** Jesus will fulfill the mystery of God on the Day of Atonement. **(Rev. 10:1-7)** The Most Holy will bring in everlasting righteousness to His people and the holy city, Jerusalem! A surviving remnant will be spiritually and physically saved after the **70th Week** is completed. **(Rom. 11:25-27)** Five days later, the Lamb and a redeemed 144,000 from the twelve tribes of Israel, will gather atop Mount Zion. **(Rev. 14:1-4)** On this day, the final harvest of believers by the Lamb will fulfill the Feast of Tabernacles! **(Rev. 14:14-16)**

Only the believers learning the events, timing, and consequences of the future **70th Week** will understand the Second Coming of Christ!

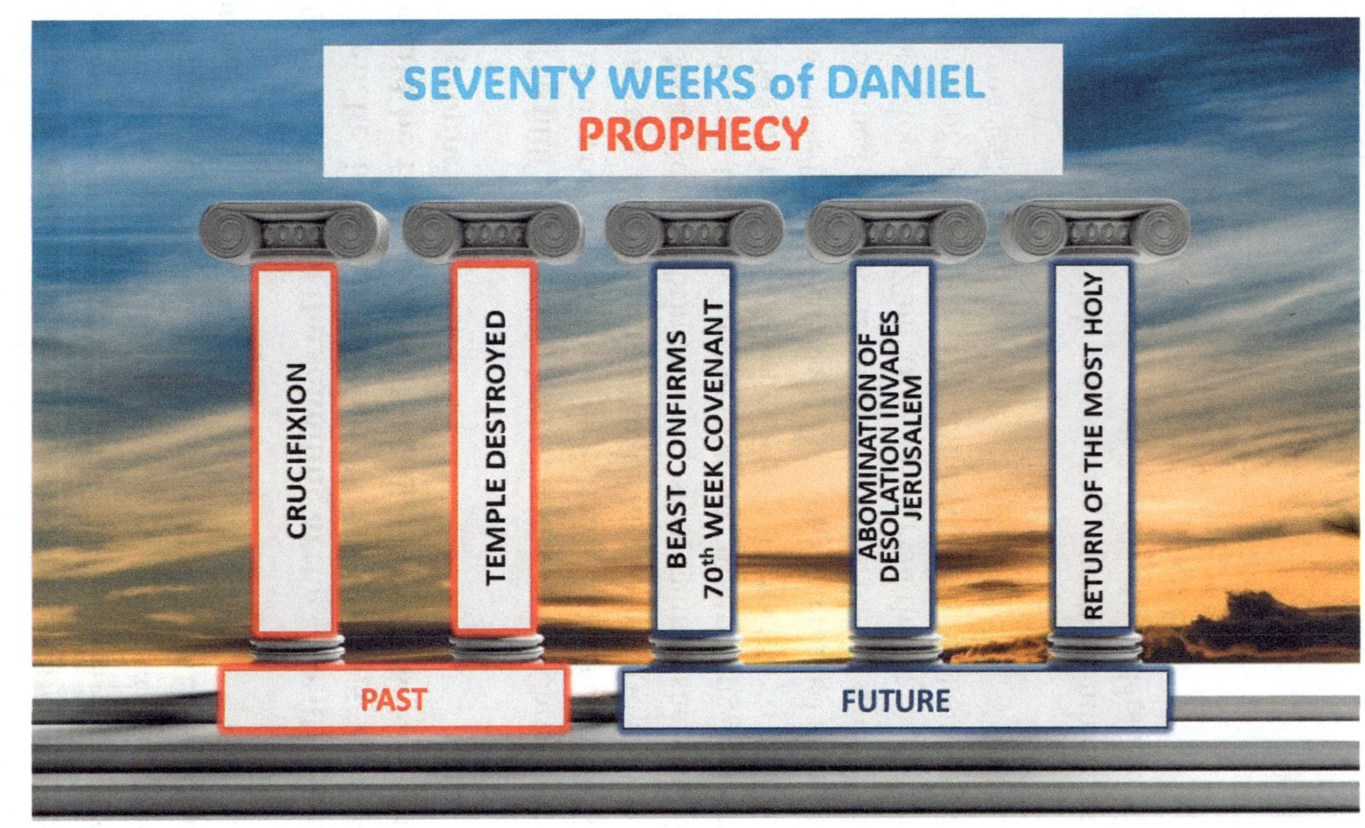
SEVENTY WEEKS of DANIEL
PROPHECY
CRUCIFIXION
TEMPLE DESTROYED
BEAST CONFIRMS 70th WEEK COVENANT
ABOMINATION OF DESOLATION INVADES JERUSALEM
RETURN OF THE MOST HOLY
PAST
FUTURE

4

The Heavenly Scroll

"Now when these things begin to happen, look up and lift up your heads, because your redemption draws near." Luke 21:28

During His ministry, Jesus foretold this amazing truth. **(Luke 9:27)** John will see the Son of Man coming in His kingdom before tasting death. Jesus later exhorted His close friend to watch for the events warning believers their redemption is near! **(Luke 21:28)** The specific events Jesus shared while on the Mount of Olives, John actually saw in The Revelation of Jesus Christ! **(Mat. 24:3-33, Rev. 6:1-17; 7:9-17)**

"Assuredly, I say to you, this generation will by no means pass away till all things take place." Luke 21:32

In this late hour, the church is in great danger. Christians are not understanding the consequences of the **70th Week**! **(Luke 21:32)** Most have never been taught this future prophecy. (**Dan. 9:24-27)** Nor the events taking place inside this seven-year period! So why should we be watching for these events? **(Mark 13:35)**

"But he who endures to the end shall be saved." Matthew 24:13

Tragically, many believers refusing to watch will not endure till the end, the harvest. **(Mat. 24:13; 13:39-42)** So, let's begin by studying the events taking place before, during, and after the Coming of The Son of Man. The goal of this chapter is to understand the timing and the consequences of these events.

"So you also, when you see all these things, know that it is near—at the doors!" Matthew 24:33

Jesus places these events inside the future **70th Week** of Daniel!
(1) The events of the Beginning of Sorrows.
(Mat. 24:4-8, Rev. 6:1-6)
(2) The events of the Great Tribulation.
(Mat. 24:9-26, Rev. 6:7-11)
(3) The constellations losing their light.
(Mat. 24:29, Rev. 6:12-17)
(4) The Son of Man coming back.
(Mat. 24:30-31, Rev. 7:9-17)
(5) The Day of The Lord erupts the same day.
(Mat. 24:37-39, Rev. 8:1-5)

And Jesus answered and said to them: "Take heed that no one deceives you. For many will come in My name, saying, 'I am the Christ,' and will deceive many. And you will hear of wars and rumors of wars. See that you are not troubled; for all these things must come to pass, but the end is not yet. For nation will rise against nation, and kingdom against kingdom. And there will be famines, pestilences, and earthquakes in various places. All these are the beginning of sorrows." Matthew 24:4-8

(1) Jesus began with this warning. Everyone should be watching for these birth pains in the first half of the future **70th Week**. Many teachers no longer abiding in Christ will deceive many believers. **(Mat. 24:4-5)** After this, wars and rumors of wars will illicit fear around the world. **(Mat. 24:6)** The addition of famines, earthquakes, and pestilences will bring the wicked to their knees. **(Mat. 24:7)** Jesus calls these events, the **Beginning of Sorrows**. **(Mat. 24:8)**

"For then there will be great tribulation, such as has not been since the beginning of the world until this time, no, nor ever shall be. And unless those days were shortened, no flesh would be saved; but for the elect's sake those days will be shortened."
Matthew 24:21-22

(2) The hard labor, the **Great Tribulation**, will begin the second half of the **70th Week. (Mat. 24:9-26)** Like in the

days of Noah, all worshipping the Beast will be living in peace and safety. **(Luke 17:26-30, 1 Thes. 5:3)** Those refusing to obey will suffer persecution never seen before. **(Mat. 24:21-22, Dan. 12:1)** The massive killing by the False Prophet will be unimaginable. **(Rev. 13:11-18)** This tribulation is also known as the **"Wrath of Satan**." **(Rev. 12:12)** For the sake of overcomers, Jesus promises to shorten (amputate) this horrific suffering. **(Rev. 7:9-17)** If not, no believers would be physically saved. This was a new revelation. Yet, His disciples recognized the next sign Jesus taught. **(Isa. 13:9-11, Mat. 24:29)**

"Immediately after the tribulation of those days the sun will be darkened, and the moon will not give its light; the stars will fall from heaven, and the powers of the heavens will be shaken." Matthew 24:29

(3) Jesus shared the sign of the Day of The Lord. **(Isa. 13:9-11, Mat. 24:29)** After the heavens lose their light, the suffering during the Great Tribulation will end. **(Mat. 24:21-22, 29, Rev. 6:12-17; 7:9-17)** Amidst this darkness, angels will gather believers from heaven and earth. **(Mark 13:24-27)**

"For as the lightning comes from the east and flashes to the west, so also will the coming of the Son of Man be...Then the sign of the Son of Man will appear in heaven, and then all the tribes of the earth will mourn..." Matthew 24:27, 30a

(4) Trapped in darkness, every eye will see the sign of the Son of Man. **(Mat. 24:27, 30a)** The wicked will mourn when they see the Son coming back in the glory of His Father! **(Rev. 1:7, Mat. 16:27)** John saw a great multitude of overcomers coming out of the Great Tribulation. They're standing before the throne of God. Gratefully thanking the Father and the Lamb for their physical salvation. **(Rev. 7:9-17)**

"...Fall on us and hide us from the face of Him who sits on the throne and from the wrath of the Lamb! For the great day of His wrath has come, and who is able to stand?" Revelation 6:16-17

(5) On this same day, the wrath of the Lamb will be poured out on the wicked left behind! **(Rev. 6:16-17; 8:1-2)** The prophets call this, the Day of The Lord. **(Isa. 13:9-11, Mat. 24:37-39, Rev. 8:2; 15:1; 16:17)**

"Now learn this parable from the fig tree: When its branch has already become tender and puts forth leaves, you know that summer is near. So you also, when you see all these things, know that it is near—at the doors!" Matthew 24:32-33

After sharing the above events, Jesus taught a parable about His Second Coming. When a fig tree puts forth leaves, the summer is near. In the same way, the overcomers living during the Great Tribulation will know when the Coming of The Son of Man is near. **(Mat. 24:30-33)**

'He who overcomes shall be clothed in white garments, and I will not blot out his name from the Book of Life; but I will confess his name before My Father and before His angels.' Revelation 3:5

The goal in, **AFTER THE SIXTH SEAL**, is to make disciples capable of overcoming till the harvest! To achieve this we need to understand the events Jesus taught John! I will use a five-question format for each event!

What is this event?
Who is involved?
When will it happen?
How will it happen?
Why will it matter?

As you study you will see these events unfold through the eyes of John. May this prepare you to faithfully stand before the Son of Man. **(Luke 21:36)**

The 70th Week of Daniel
The Three Time Periods
Matthew 24; Revelation 6-8

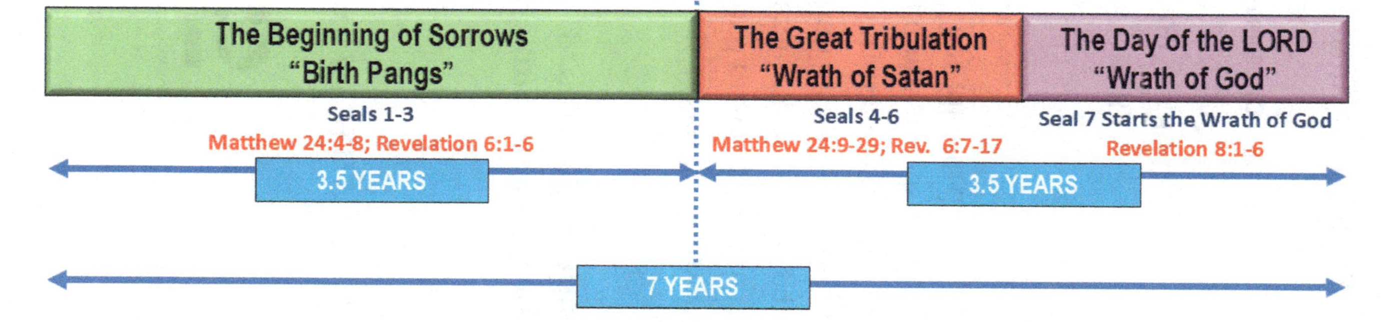

5

The Little Horn: At Any Moment

"I was watching; and the same horn was making war against the saints, and prevailing against them." Daniel 7:21

Throughout history, Satan has failed to destroy the people that gave us the Christ! His evil plan began with the Pharaoh of Egypt. The children of Israel never would have survived without the divine intervention by God! This did not stop the Devil from trying again. So far, the enemy has manipulated the leaders of seven kingdoms (heads). His plan is to annihilate the Jewish race. They all failed!

<u>SEVEN HEADS</u>

1. Pharaoh of Egypt in 1450 B.C.
2. Shalmaneser of Assyria in 722 B.C.
3. Nebuchadnezzar of Babylon in 586 B.C.
4. Xerxes of Medo-Persia in 536 B.C.
5. Alexander the Great of Greece in 330 B.C.
6. Domitian of Rome in 96 A.D.
7. Adolph Hitler of Nazi Germany in 1939-1945

‘The beast…is himself also the eighth, and is of the seven, and is going to perdition.’ Revelation 17:11

The seventh head killed more Jews than the previous six combined. Yet, there is a future leader, the eighth head, who will be greater than Hitler. John calls him the Beast! **(Rev. 13:1; 17:11)**

‘And it shall come to pass in all the land,” Says the LORD, “That two-thirds in it shall be cut off and die, But one-third shall be left in it: I will bring the one-third through the fire, Will refine them as silver is refined, And test them as gold is tested. ,They will call on My name, And I will answer them. I will say, ‘This is My people’; And each one will say, ‘The LORD is my God.’” Zechariah 13:8-9

On October 7th, 2023, Muslim terrorists crossed over the Israeli border. Within hours they murdered over 1,200 men, women, and children. The mysterious Beast was watching. He will have fierce features. **(Dan. 8:23-24)** Satan is waiting to give this world leader His power over the nations! **(Rev. 13:2-7)** Their goal is clear. This evil man will cut off and kill two-thirds of Israel. **(Zech. 13:8-9)**

What is this event?

Remember therefore how you have received and heard; hold fast and repent. Therefore if you will not watch, I will come upon you as a thief, and you will not know what hour I will come upon you.” Revelation 3:3

Most have been taught since Israel became a nation, there are no more events left to watch for. This is why so many are convinced the resurrection of believers can happen at any moment. Nothing could be further from the truth! **(Rev. 17:12-13)** Why should we learn the events warning us His Coming is near? **(Mat. 24:33)** For all refusing to watch, Jesus will come as a thief. **(1 Thes. 5:1-4)** At the harvest, only the overcomers will stand before the Son of Man. **(Luke 21:36, Rev. 7:9-17)**

'Then he shall confirm a covenant with many for one week...' Daniel 9:27a

Daniel saw in a night vision a leader speaking pompous words. His plan is to confirm a seven-year covenant of peace between Israel and many Muslims. **(Dan. 9:27a)** This deceiver has several names in scripture.
Daniel calls him, the Little Horn. **(Dan. 7:8)**
Jesus calls him, the Abomination of Desolation. **(Mat. 24:15)**
Paul calls him, the Man of Sin. **(2 Thes. 2:3-4)**
John calls him, the Beast. **(Rev. 13:1)**
Believers may call him, the Antichrist! **(1 John 2:22)**

"The ten horns which you saw are ten kings who have received no kingdom as yet, but they receive authority for one hour as kings with the beast. These are of one mind, and they will give their power and authority to the beast."
Revelation 17:12-13

So, what's the next event on Gods end time calendar? A warning sign every Christian should recognize. The Little Horn (Beast) is going to visit the Middle East. **(Dan. 7:7-8, 20)** His goal is to gain the trust of ten Arab nations (horns) surrounding Israel. The kings from these nations will eventually give their authority and power to the Beast. **(Rev. 17:12-13)** After this, this deceiver will confirm a peace covenant with Israel. **(Dan. 9:27a)** The world will be shocked. Over the years, many have failed to deliver peace to the Jewish people. Only this time, the wicked will blindly be witnessing bible prophecy. The **70th Week** will begin the moment the Beast confirms a seven year covenant between Israel and her surrounding enemies. These ten nations will agree to peacefully coexist with the Jewish people.

'And in the latter time of their kingdom, When the transgressors have reached their fullness, A king shall arise, Having fierce features, Who understands sinister schemes.' Daniel 8:23

In this late hour, Satan has sent forth demons with a specific assignment. It's not what you think. The Devil wants you to believe the lie: *"We should all be looking for Jesus; not the Antichrist!"* Why is the enemy doing this? The many trusting in this deception won't recognize the Beast while he gains the support of leaders from ten Arab nations (horns). **(Rev. 17:12-13)** Once the Antichrist invades the Middle East we will see how many Christians are living in darkness! **(Dan. 7:7-8, 20; 8:23)**

Who is involved?

'The ten horns are ten kings Who shall arise from this kingdom. And another shall rise after them; He shall be different from the first ones, and shall subdue three kings.' Daniel 7:24

The enemies of the Jewish people will be captivated by the power of the Beast. **(Rev. 13:4)** That is until he confronts resistance from three Muslim nations (horns). **(Dan. 7:24)** At first, their leaders (kings) will ignore his threats to obey. In retaliation, they will announce they have no intention of laying down their weapons. **(Dan. 7:20)**

When will it happen?

"And the ten horns that were on its head, and the other horn which came up, before which three fell, namely, that horn which had eyes and a mouth which spoke pompous words, whose appearance was greater than his fellows.' Daniel 7:20

The Little Horn (Beast) will grow in power after gaining the support of ten nations surrounding the Glorious Land. **(Rev. 17:12-13, Dan. 8:9)** While forcing three Muslim nations to stop attacking Israel **(Dan. 7:20)**, seven more Muslim leaders will agree to coexist with the Jewish people. **(Rev. 17:12-13)** We aren't told how long it will take for the Beast to control all ten nations. **(Dan. 7:7-8)** So, when can we expect to see this happen? The assault of three defiant Muslim nations by the Little Horn (Beast) can take place at any moment. **(Dan. 7:20)**

How will it happen?

'And out of one of them came a little horn which grew exceedingly great toward the south, toward the east, and toward the Glorious Land.' Daniel 8:9

How will the enemies of the Jewish people react after a pompous leader, the Little Horn, plucks out the roots of three Muslim nations? **(Dan. 7:8)** These brutal attacks will convince the leaders of seven more Muslim nations to support his peace proposal with Israel. **(Rev. 17:12-13)** What about the Christians supporting this seven year covenant? **(Dan. 9:27b)** Such blindness is from the enemy! Satan will be targeting those refusing to obey the Spirit of God! Even when presented with the scriptures, many will not understand. It will be a different story for the overcomers! **(Rev. 7:9-17)** When the world begins to worship the Beast during the Great Tribulation **(Mat. 24:21-22, Rev. 13:1-18)**, the faithful will be ready to overcome by the blood of the Lamb and the word of their testimony. **(Rev. 3:5; 12:11-12)**

"Behold, I am coming as a thief. Blessed is he who watches, and keeps his garments, lest he walk naked and they see his shame." Revelation 16:15

We often hear, *"The Great Tribulation is only for the Jews!"* (False)

Paul taught the Man of Sin will be revealed in the middle of the **70th Week.** This will initiate the days of the Great Tribulation before our gathering to Jesus at His Coming. **(2 Thes. 2:1-4)** Then why are so many refusing to watch for the Beast? It's because they believe the **70th Week** is only for Israel. **(Dan. 9:24)** I emphasize again, by quoting Daniel **(Dan. 9:27a, Mat. 24:15)**, Jesus places inside the second half of the **70th Week**:

The events of the Great Tribulation. **(Mat. 24:9-26)**

The Coming of The Son of Man. **(Mat. 24:27-31)**

The beginning of the Day of The Lord. **(Mat. 24:37-39)**

Which means God will deal with the church and unsaved Israel during the Great Tribulation! **(Mat. 24:15-39)** We aren't told how many Christians will be martyred by the Beast. **(Rev. 6:9-11, Rev. 20:4)** We do know over two thirds of Israel will be cut off and killed during the second half of the **70th Week**! **(Zech. 13:8-9)**

Why will it matter?

"Through his cunning He shall cause deceit to prosper under his rule; And he shall exalt himself in his heart. He shall destroy many in their prosperity. He shall even rise against the Prince of princes; But he shall be broken without human means."
Daniel 8:25

The world will be watching as this mysterious leader carries out his plan. Many will praise the wisdom of the Muslim leaders agreeing to live peacefully alongside the Jewish people! **(Rev. 17:12-13)** Spirit-led believers will understand this dangerous hour. **(Dan. 8:25)** They will recognize the identity of the Beast, his nation, and the leaders of ten Arab nations (horns) giving him their power. They will also be ready for the next event, the beginning of the **70th Week** of Daniel! **(Dan. 9:27)**

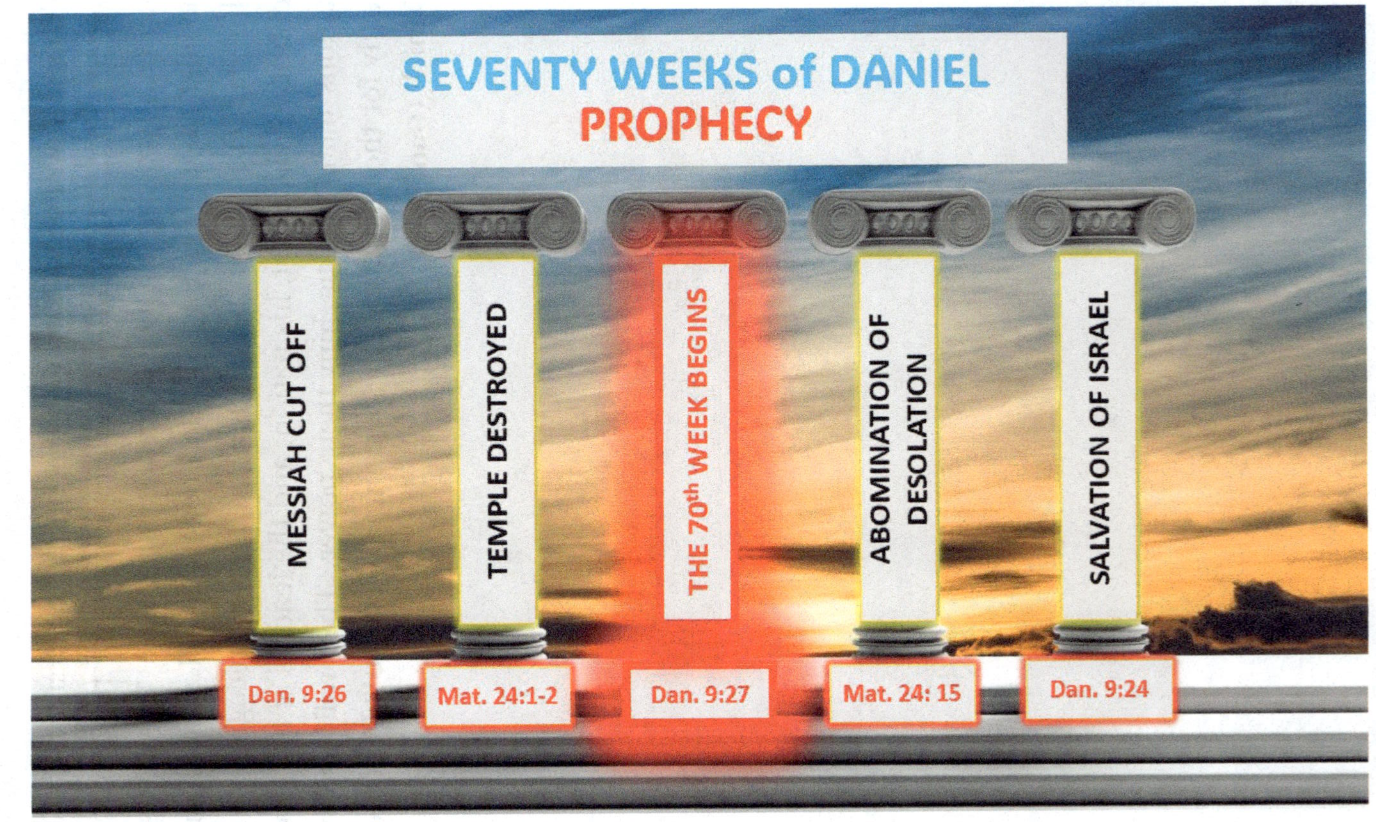

SEVENTY WEEKS of DANIEL
PROPHECY
MESSIAH CUT OFF
Dan. 9:26
TEMPLE DESTROYED
Mat. 24:1-2
THE 70th WEEK BEGINS
Dan. 9:27
ABOMINATION OF DESOLATION
Mat. 24: 15
SALVATION OF ISRAEL
Dan. 9:24

6

The 70th Week of Daniel

'Seventy weeks are determined for your people and for your holy city, to finish the transgression, to make an end of sins, to make reconciliation for iniquity, to bring in everlasting righteousness, to seal up vision and prophecy, And to anoint the Most Holy.' Daniel 9:24

Israel is the size of New Jersey. The population is 9,797,000. Surrounding her are twenty-one Arab nations. Their leaders are convinced the Jews have stolen their land. This is why a permanent truce is not possible. Many will be skeptical when a pompous leader arrives promising to broker peace. So what is preventing the destruction of the Jewish people? **(Dan. 10:14)** Like Israel becoming a nation in 1948, cvcry eye will witness the **70th Week** of Daniel prophecy. **(Dan. 9:24)**

What is this event?

"Now I have come to make you understand what will happen to your people in the latter days, for the vision refers to many days yet to come." Daniel 10:14

The angel Gabriel foretold this prophecy concerning the future salvation of Israel. **(Dan. 9:24-27)** Daniels people were sinning with no intention of repenting. Due to their refusal to obey, God decreed a future chastisement upon the Jewish people. For seventy weeks, Israel will be dominated by her enemies (70x7=490 years). The purpose of this discipline is to give the Jewish people an opportunity to repent of their rejection of the Messiah! This prophecy began after Nehemiah was given the command to restore the gates of the temple and the wall of Jerusalem. **(Neh. 2:5-8)** Four hundred and eighty-three years later (69 Weeks), Jesus was crucified. After almost two thousand years, the Most Holy will be anointed on the Day of Atonement. **(Dan. 9:24)** The Christ will return a second time and save a surviving remnant believing in Him! **(Heb. 9:28, Rev. 10:1-7)** This will be the fulfillment of the **70th Week,** an event a Christ rejecting world will witness! **(Dan. 10:14)**

Who is involved?

'... And there, in this horn, were eyes like the eyes of a man, and a mouth speaking pompous words.' Daniel 7:8

Who will be involved before the **70th Week** of Daniel is confirmed? **(Dan. 9:27a)** The Beast (Little Horn) will begin by gathering the support from the leaders of ten Arab nations surrounding Israel. **(Rev. 17:12-13)** Three of these horns attacking the Jewish people will refuse to comply with his vision of peace. The Little Horn will respond by plucking the roots out of these nations. **(Dan. 7:7-8, 20)** We aren't told how long it will take before the leaders of these nations agree to surrender. Or how much time will elapse before the Beast confirms the **70th Week** covenant with Israel. **(Dan. 9:27a)** One can imagine the reaction after witnessing this ceremony in Jerusalem. A picture of a smiling Prime Minister of Israel standing with the leaders of ten Muslim nations. **(Rev. 17:12-13)** And who is between them? The most wicked person ever born! **(Dan. 7:11)** Muslims will be honoring Allah while Jewish rabbis will be praising Jehovah. Christian leaders will be declaring this pompous leader a messenger from God! We may hear echoing through the streets, "It's the miracle of miracles!" Such blindness to bible prophecy will be a sign the **70th Week** is underway! May we never underestimate the warfare we will experience after this covenant is confirmed. Especially, after telling everyone the deceiver the world is admiring is the Antichrist! **(Rev. 13:3-4, 1 John 2:18)**

When will it happen?

"And in the latter time of their kingdom, when the transgressors have reached their fullness, a king shall arise. Having fierce features, who understands sinister schemes. His power shall be mighty, but not by his own power He shall destroy fearfully, And shall prosper and thrive. He shall destroy the mighty, and also the holy people." Daniel 8:23-24

The world will be rejoicing the moment the Beast confirms the peace with Israel. **(Dan. 9:27a)** This is when discerning Christians will recognize his true identity and his evil mission. **(Dan. 8:23-24)** Forty-two months later, the armies of the Beast will break this covenant by surrounding an unsuspecting Jerusalem. **(Luke 21:20)** On this day, the Man of Sin (Beast) will exalt himself in the temple of God! **(2 Thes. 2:3-4)** He will be called the abomination that causes desolation after placing an image of himself inside the holy place. **(Mat. 24:15, Rev. 13:9-18)** This is an expression for worshiping an idol in the place of God. This same day the world will choose to worship the Beast and Satan! The beginning of the Great Tribulation. **(Rev. 13:4)**

How will it happen?

'For I do not desire, brethren, that you should be ignorant of this mystery, lest you should be wise in your own opinion, that blindness in part has happened to Israel until the fullness of the Gentiles has come in. And so all Israel will be saved...' Romans 11:25-26

Paul is warning us not to be ignorant of this mystery. **(Rom. 11:25-27)** After the **70th Week** ends, the Christ will physically return a second time on the **Day of Atonement**. **(Heb. 9:28)** The Most Holy will begin by removing Israel's blindness to His gospel! **(Dan. 9:24)** Later, during the **Feast of Tabernacles**, all believing in Jesus will be physically saved. **(Rev. 14:1-4, 14-16)**

'But in the days of the sounding of the seventh angel, when he is about to sound, the mystery of God would be finished, as He declared to His servants the prophets.' Revelation 10:7

After the **70th Week** is completed, the Most Holy will physically return for the salvation of Israel. **(Dan. 9:24)** In his vision, John saw the Christ fulfill the mystery of God. **(Rev. 10:1-7)** This miracle of salvation will take place on the Day of Atonement. **(Rom. 11:25-27)** Every year this holy Feast is honored in the fall (Sept/Oct). Which means the world will watch the Beast confirm this covenant with Israel in the fall of the year. Seven years later, every eye will see the Christ save a remnant eagerly waiting for Him on the Day of Atonement. **(Heb. 9:28)**

'These are the feasts of the Lord, holy convocations which you shall proclaim at their appointed times.' Leviticus 23:4

I emphasize again, knowing the timing of these holy convocations is the key to understanding the events, timing, and consequences of the Second Coming of Christ. The mystery of the resurrection will take place during the **Feast of Trumpets**. **(1 Cor. 15:50-52, Mat. 24:29-36)** After the opening of the **Sixth Seal**, a great multitude of believers will be taken out of the **Great Tribulation** and stand before the throne of God in heaven. **(Rev. 7:9-17)** No one will know the day or hour the constellations will lose their light during this holy Feast. **(Mark 13:24-27)**

"I will bring the one-third through the fire, will refine them as silver is refined, and test them as gold is tested. They will call on My name, and I will answer them. I will say, 'This is My people'; and each one will say, 'The Lord is my God.' " Zechariah 13:9

The Most Holy will fulfill the mystery of God between the **Sixth** and **Seventh Trumpets**. **(Rev. 10:7)** The Christ will take away the sins of one third of Israel on the Day of Atonement. **(Heb. 9:28, Rom. 11:26-27, Zech. 13:8-9)** Five days later, the final harvest of believers will fulfill the Feast of Tabernacles. **(Rev. 14:1-4; 14:14-16)**

<u>Why will it matter?</u>

"Therefore when you see the 'abomination of desolation,' spoken of by Daniel the prophet, standing in the holy place" (whoever reads, let him understand)." Matthew 24:15

Why did Jesus quote Daniel while on the Mount of Olives? **(Dan. 9:27, Luke 21:20)** Our Lord is exhorting us to recognize the Abomination of Desolation after he stands in the holy place. **(Mat. 24:15)** Only the overcomers will understand the consequences of this blasphemy during the second half of the **70th Week.**

"But when you see Jerusalem surrounded by armies, then know that its desolation is near.'
Luke 21:20

1) The Great Tribulation will begin the day the Beast surrounds Jerusalem with his armies. **(Mat. 24:15-22, Luke 21:20)** After blaspheming God, the Man of Sin will be called the Abomination of Desolation! **(Rev. 13:6, 2 Thes. 2:3-4)**

'The sun and moon will grow dark, And the stars will diminish their brightness.' Joel 3:15

2) The day the heavens lose their light during the **Feast of Trumpets** **(Joel 3:15, Mat. 24:29, 36, Rev. 6:12-17)** the Son will send forth angels to gather dead and alive believers before the throne of God. **(Mark 13:24-27, 1 Thes. 4:15-17)**

'But in the days of the sounding of the seventh angel, when he is about to sound, the mystery of God would be finished, as He declared to His servants the prophets.' Revelation 10:7

3) After the **70th Week** is completed, the Most Holy will fulfill the mystery of God. **(Dan. 9:24, Rev. 10:1-7)** The Christ will save a faithful remnant on the **Day of Atonement**. **(Heb. 9:28, Rom. 11:25-27)** During the **Feast of Tabernacles**, the Lamb will complete the final harvest of born again Jews. **(Rev. 14:1-4, 14-16)**

"I have not sent these prophets, yet they ran. I have not spoken to them, yet they prophesied."
Jeremiah 23:21

Why are Christians struggling to understand the events Jesus will fulfill during His Second Coming? **(John 14:26)** Rather than being taught by the Holy Spirit, they're trusting in the prophecies of false teachers. **(Jer. 23:21)** How so? Many are convinced the **Feasts of The Lord** are past. Clearly, this is not from the Holy Spirit. No one is going to prevent the Messiah from fulfilling the mystery of God during His Second Coming! **(Rom. 11:25-27, Rev. 10:1-7)**

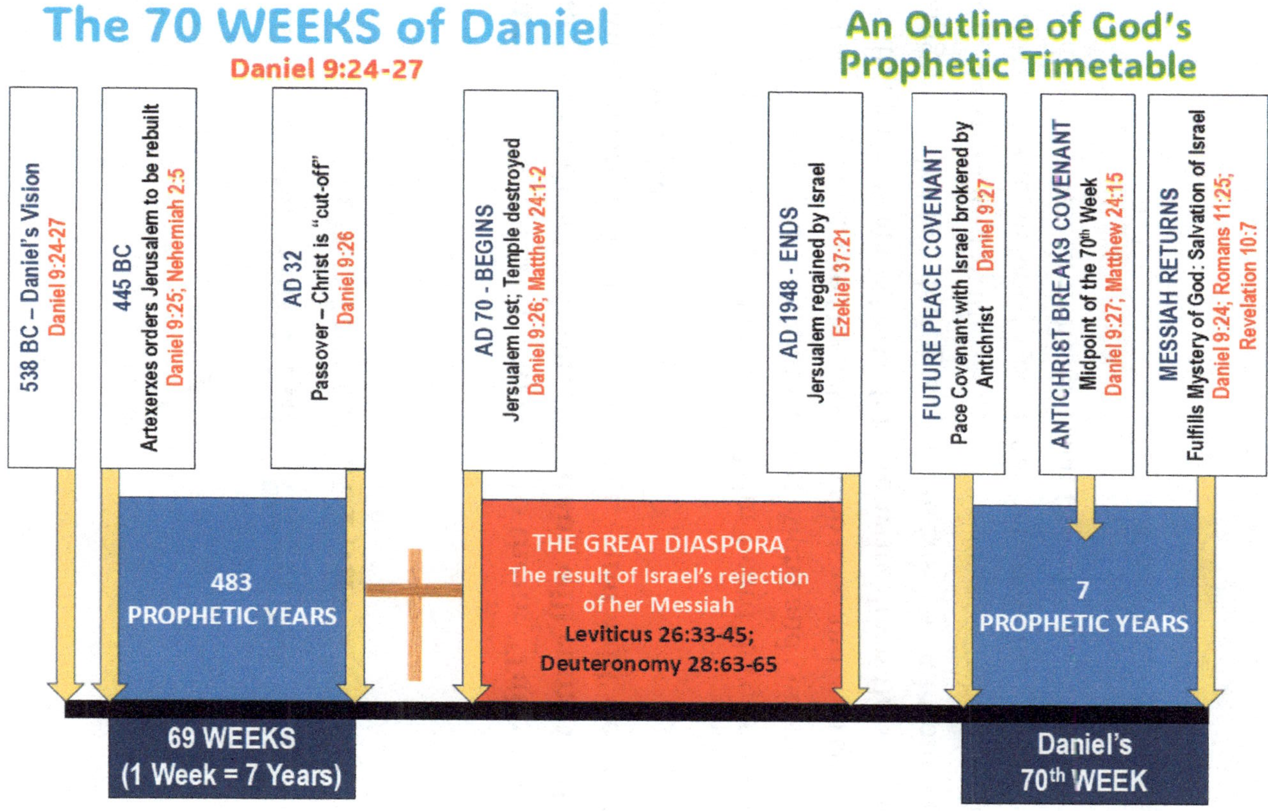

The 70 WEEKS of Daniel
Daniel 9:24-27
An Outline of God's Prophetic Timetable
538 BC – Daniel's Vision
Daniel 9:24-27
445 BC
Artexerxes orders Jerusalem to be rebuilt
Daniel 9:25; Nehemiah 2:5
AD 32
Passover – Christ is "cut-off"
Daniel 9:26
AD 70 - BEGINS
Jersualem lost; Temple destroyed
Daniel 9:26; Matthew 24:1-2
AD 1948 - ENDS
Jersualem regained by Israel
Ezekiel 37:21
FUTURE PEACE COVENANT
Pace Covenant with Israel brokered by Antichrist Daniel 9:27
ANTICHRIST BREAKS COVENANT
Midpoint of the 70th Week
Daniel 9:27; Matthew 24:15
MESSIAH RETURNS
Fulfills Mystery of God: Salvation of Israel
Daniel 9:24; Romans 11:25; Revelation 10:7
483
PROPHETIC YEARS
THE GREAT DIASPORA
The result of Israel's rejection of her Messiah
Leviticus 26:33-45;
Deuteronomy 28:63-65
7
PROPHETIC YEARS
69 WEEKS
(1 Week = 7 Years)
Daniel's
70th WEEK

7

First Seal: Take Heed No One Deceives You

'And Jesus answered and said to them: "Take heed that no one deceives you. For many will come in My name, saying, 'I am the Christ,' and will deceive many. Matthew 24:4-5

It was on the Lords Day when John heard a voice from behind. Standing before him was the Alpha and Omega, the First and the Last! The One who is, who was, and is to come, the Almighty! Jesus exhorts John to write down the events taking place before, during and after His Second Coming! **(Rev. 1:19)** Before witnessing these events ushering in eternity, John listened as Jesus shared the spiritual condition of seven churches in Asia! **(Rev. 1:11)**

"I am the Alpha and the Omega, the First and the Last," and, "What you see, write in a book and send it to the seven churches which are in Asia: to Ephesus, to Smyrna, to Pergamos, to Thyatira, to Sardis, to Philadelphia, and to Laodicea."
Revelation 1:11

Our Lord began by revealing the spiritual decay of the above churches. **(Rev. 1:11)** His explicit language was not just to expose their sins. Jesus was offering forgiveness to believers who will repent. It must have been painful for John to write down such powerful exhortations. Especially because the spiritual condition of these first century believers is a painful reflection of the body of Christ in these last days! At this moment, many have lost their first love. **(Rev. 2:1-7)** While others have no intention of exposing the false doctrines infecting their churches. **(Rev. 2:14-15)** Or righteously judging Christians committing sexual immorality. **(Rev. 2:20-23)** We have all seen the rapid growth of mega churches claiming to be on fire for God. Yet, in the eyes of God they're dead! **(Rev. 3:2-3)** And finally, the increase of believers professing to be rich and need of nothing! Jesus calls them wretched, miserable, poor, blind, and naked. **(Rev. 3:14-22)** If they don't repent, they will be lost for eternity! What is the Spirit saying to us? **(Rev. 3:5)** Only the overcomers will sit with the Son on His throne! **(Rev. 3:21-22)**

‘After these things I looked, and behold, a door standing open in heaven. And the first voice which I heard was like a trumpet speaking with me, saying, “Come up here, and I will show you things which must take place after this.” Revelation 4:1

After writing down these exhortations to these seven churches, John sees an open door in heaven. **(Rev. 4:1)** A voice like a trumpet summons the apostle to come up. Immediately, he was in the spirit. Soon, in a vision, Jesus will reveal to John the resurrection of believers out of the Great Tribulation. **(Rev. 7:9-17)** Why did our Lord do this? He knew how Satan would attack in these last days. The enemy is using pastors to deceive believers on the timing of the resurrection. **(Luke 21:8)** Their lack of understanding of the harvest is not biblical nor from the Holy Spirit! **(Mat. 13:39-42; 25:31-46)** Many are actually declaring the resurrection is in Revelation 4:1. They teach John somehow represents the church being taken up to heaven. They insist the trumpet he hears is the last trump. **(1 Cor. 15:50-52)** This is why they vainly teach the church will be caught up before the opening of the **First Seal. (Rev. 6:1-2)** My friends, there is no resurrection of dead and alive believers until the Lamb opens the **Sixth Seal**! **(1 Thes. 4:15-17, Mark 13:24-27, Rev. 6:12-17)** This is the only time a great multitude of overcomers will come out of the Great Tribulation and stand before the Father and the Lamb. **(Rev. 7:9-17)** Which means anyone denying this truth is being deceived by Satan! **(Luke 21:8, Rev. 3:21:22)**

'And I saw in the right hand of Him who sat on the throne a scroll written inside and on the back, sealed with seven seals.' Revelation 5:1

While in the spirit, John saw God the Father sitting on His throne! He is holding a scroll in His right hand. It is sealed with seven seals! An angel proclaims with a loud voice, *"Who is worthy to open the scroll and loose its seals?* John wept because no one was found worthy to open the scroll and read it. **(Rev. 5:1-4)**

'But one of the elders said to me, "Do not weep. Behold, the Lion of the tribe of Judah, the Root of David, has prevailed to open the scroll and to loose its seven seals." Revelation 5:5

All of heaven saw the Lion of the tribe of Judah approach the throne. The Son received the scroll from the extended hand of His Father! **(Rev. 5:5-7)** Every eye watched as the Lamb of God opened the **First Seal**. **(Rev. 6:1-2)**

<u>What is this event?</u>

'Now I saw when the Lamb opened one of the seals; and I heard one of the four living creatures saying with a voice like thunder, "Come and see. And I looked, and behold, a white horse. He who sat on it had a bow; and a crown was given to him, and he went out conquering and to conquer.'
Revelation 6:1-2

One of the four living creatures announced, *"Come and see."* **(Rev. 6:1-2)** John looked and saw a rider sitting on a white horse. He has a bow and is wearing a crown. We aren't told his name. He is coming down to earth to conquer many believers! **(Mark 13:5-6)** This rider will achieve this by empowering teachers no longer serving Christ. These apostates will deceive many Christians during the Beginning of Sorrows! **(Mat. 24:4-8, Luke 21:8)**

'For the time will come when they will not endure sound doctrine, but according to their own desires, because they have itching ears, they will heap up for themselves teachers; and they will turn their ears away from the truth, and be turned aside to fables.' 2 Timothy 4:3-4

We have all had friends who loved God. Serving the Lord was their purpose in life! Watching them grow in their faith was a joy. Until they were captivated by false teachers bringing destructive heresies. **(2 Pet. 2:1)** Due to their itching ears, enduring sound doctrine was no longer a priority. **(2 Tim. 4:3-4)** Their refusal to continually abide in the doctrine of Christ was their downfall! **(2 John 1:9-10)** Eventually, deceiving spirits gained a stronghold in their lives. In these last days, the Spirit is warning us against believers departing from the faith by giving heed to doctrines of demons. **(1 Tim. 4:1, Heb. 6:4-6; 10:26-31)**

'And He said: "Take heed that you not be deceived. For many will come in My name, saying, 'I am He,' and, 'The time has drawn near.' Therefore do not go after them." Luke 21:8

The atmosphere for deception will be ripe the day the Lamb opens the **First Seal**. **(Rev. 6:1-2)** A time when many ministers will no longer be seeking the approval of God. The praise for their ministry will be intoxicating. Their lust for the approval of man will be great. They will attract a greater following by prophesying His Coming is drawing near, at any moment. **(Luke 21:8)** At the same time, they will convince many to support his covenant of death with Israel. **(Isa. 28:18)**

'Of how much worse punishment, do you suppose, will he be thought worthy who has trampled the Son of God underfoot, counted the blood of the covenant by which he was sanctified a common thing, and insulted the Spirit of grace?' Hebrews 10:29

Imagine being sanctified by the blood of Jesus, while choosing to trample the Son of God underfoot. **(Heb. 10:26-29)** Believers so crippled they will no longer be able to hear from God! **(Mat. 13:39-41)** Sadly, the rider of the white horse will target those insulting the Spirit of grace! **(Rev. 6:1-2**

Who is involved?

"For God has put it into their hearts to fulfill His purpose, to be of one mind, and to give their kingdom to the beast, until the words of God are fulfilled." Revelation 17:17

John was in the spirit when he arrives in heaven. **(Rev. 4:1)** His vision of events taking place before the Coming of The Son of Man is underway. He saw the kings of ten nations giving their power to the Beast! For God has put it in their hearts to give their kingdom to the Beast until the words of God are fulfilled. **(Rev. 17:12-17)**

'And Jesus answered and said to them: "Take heed that no one deceives you. For many will come in My name, saying, 'I am the Christ,' and will deceive many." Matthew 24:4-5

The **70th Week** of Daniel will begin the moment the Beast confirms the false peace. **(Dan. 9:27a)** The world will be celebrating how this courageous leader has miraculously reconciled such bitter enemies. That same day, the Lamb will open the **First Seal** of the heavenly scroll. **(Rev. 6:1-2)** Amidst this festivity a rider on a white horse will arrive on earth. An event most Christians will not be expecting. A time when many apostates will arise and deceive many believers! **(Mat. 24:4-5)** They will boldly declare this mediator is a messenger sent by God. They will insist bringing peace to Jerusalem is an answer to prayer. This is why they will persecute anyone calling him the Antichrist! How bad could it be? Such denial will create the worst division in the history of the church. **(Mat. 24:9-14)** Many supporting this popular leader have already made up their minds. It won't matter how many scriptures you show them! **(Rev. 13:1-18)** For those refusing to repent of such idolatry, their eternal fate is before them! **(Rev. 14:9-11)** They will pave the way for the Beast to overcome many saints. **(Rev. 13:7, 2 Thes. 2:1-4)** This will be a wakeup call for those wanting to endure till the harvest! **(Mat. 24:13, 13:39)** Christians will have two choices. They can follow these deceptive wolves posing as sheep. **(Mat. 7:15)** Or they can overcome them by obeying the Holy Spirit during the Great Tribulation. **(Rom. 15:13, Rev. 7:9-17)**

When will it happen?

'Then he shall confirm a covenant with many for one week...' Daniel 9:27

So when can we expect to see the **70th Week**? Two events will initiate this seven year prophecy. The same day the Beast confirms a covenant of death between Jews and Muslims, the rider on the white horse will begin conquering believers. **(Dan. 9:27, Rev. 6:1-2)** The saints supporting the Beast will be obvious. **(Rev. 13:7)** To be clear, the opening of the **First Seal** by the Lamb will initiate the Beginning of Sorrows, the first half of the **70th Week**. **(Rev. 6:1-2, Mat. 24:8)**

"For nation will rise against nation, and kingdom against kingdom. And there will be earthquakes in various places, and there will be famines and troubles. These are the beginnings of sorrows." Mark 13:8

Then why are most Christians refusing to watch for the events from the first three seals? Sadly, they're convinced they will be caught up to heaven before the **70th Week** erupts. **(Mark 13:8, Rev. 6:1-6)** The truth is, Jesus will gather believers from heaven and earth only after the constellations lose their light. **(Mark 13:24-27)** The prophets call this the sign of The Day of The Lord! **(Isa. 13:9-11, Joel 2:30-31)**

'For what have I to do with judging those also who are outside? Do you not judge those who are inside? But those who are outside God judges. Therefore "put away from yourselves the evil person."
1 Corinthians 5:12-13

Paul's exhortation to judge the sins of believers is rarely heard today. **(1 Cor. 5:11-13)** Instead, many are teaching Satan's lie, *"Only God can judge."* This is why so many believers are becoming tares! **(Mat. 13:39-42)** Such apostasy is due to preachers insisting we should love and not judge. I ask you, why is righteously judging from their pulpits no longer an option? **(John 7:24)** It's because happiness, not holiness, is the cornerstone of the fastest growing churches in the world! This is why so many believers will refuse to righteously judge the Beast! **(Rev. 13:4)**

<u>How will it happen?</u>

"...And all the world marveled and followed the beast. So they worshiped the dragon who gave authority to the beast; and they worshiped the beast, saying, "Who is like the beast? Who is able to make war with him?" Revelation 13:3b-4

How will saints conform with the world during the 70th Week? **(James 4:4)** Well known bible teachers will blindly declare his covenant with Israel is a vote for peace. They will insist he is a vessel sent by God. **(Mat. 24:4-5)** In their eyes no one can successfully war against Him. **(Rev. 13:4-6)** In the end, it won't matter what blasphemies this pompous leader speaks. So how will the Beast overcome saints during the Great Tribulation? By the authority Satan gives him! **(Rev. 13:2, 7)**

'Who have strayed concerning the truth, saying that the resurrection is already past; and they overthrow the faith of some.' 2 Timothy 2:18

After the peace with Israel is confirmed, the preservation of self during the Beginning of Sorrows will become a top priority. Teachers having strayed from the truth will overthrow the faith of believers by prophesying the resurrection is past. Beware saints! They will say anything to conceal the identity of the Beast before the world receives his mark during the Great Tribulation! **(Rev. 13:1-18; 14:9-11)**

'I have set watchmen on your walls, O Jerusalem; They shall never hold their peace day or night. You who make mention of the Lord, do not keep silent.' Isaiah 62:6

On the first day of the **70th Week**, most Christians will have no idea they're being deceived! **(Mark 13:23-27)** To warn them, the Holy Spirit will raise up Watchmen refusing to be silent. **(Isa. 62:6)** These overcomers will begin by revealing the evil mission of the Beast! **(Rev. 13:1-18)** The attacks against them will be swift. The unfaithful tares will accuse them of slander! **(Mat. 13:39-42)** They will insist this pompous leader is God's anointed! Before long, the warnings by the Watchmen will be drowned out. Even so, no one abiding in Christ will support the Beast!

Why will it matter?

'Then you shall again discern, Between the righteous and the wicked, between one who serves God, and one who does not serve Him.' Malachi 3:18

The rising apostasy after the **First Seal** is just the beginning. **(2 Thes. 2:3-4, Mat. 24:4-5, Rev. 6:1-2)** Preparing for this event, Satan has already sown many tares among the wheat. **(Mat. 13:39-42)** The wicked no longer serving God will blur the words of the righteous. (**Mal. 3:18)** Their approval of the Beast will be a red flag to the overcomers. **(Rev. 13:6)** And how will you react when faced with criticism from the followers of the Beast? Which may include your pastor, church members, close friends, even members from your own family? Sadly, those not willing to overcome will deny their Lord by remaining silent.

"So when you see the 'abomination of desolation, spoken of by Daniel the prophet, standing where it ought not" (let the reader understand), "then let those who are in Judea flee to the mountains." Mark 13:14

So what will be the goal of the rider of the white horse? His mission is to prevent anyone from understanding the timing and the consequences of the Beginning of Sorrows **(Mat. 24:8)**, the Great Tribulation **(Mat. 24:21-22)**, the Coming of the Son of Man **(Mat. 24:27-31)**, and the beginning of the Day of The Lord! **(Mat. 24:37-39)** By quoting the prophet Daniel, Jesus places these events inside the future **70th Week**. **(Mat. 24:15, Mark 13:14, Luke 21:20)**

The BEGINNING OF SORROWS
The First Seal

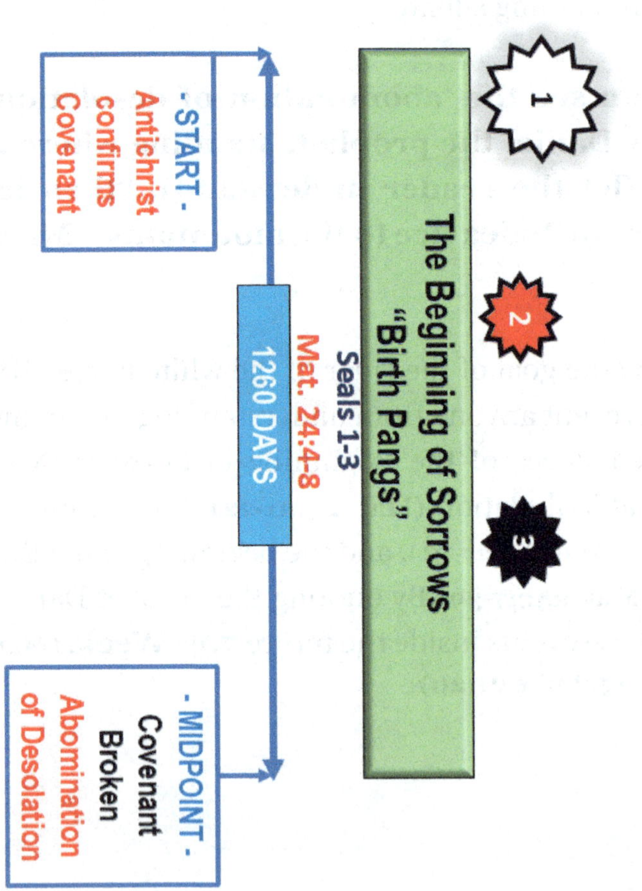

8

Second Seal: Nation Against Nation

'Then He said to them, "Nation will rise against nation, and kingdom against kingdom." Luke 21:10

The day the Beast confirms the seven year peace covenant between Israel and her enemies **(Dan. 9:27a)**, popular teachers will begin deceiving many Christians. **(Mat. 24:4-5, Rev. 6:1-2)** At the same time, an astonished world will be captivated with Jerusalem. Miraculously, Israel will finally be living in peace! The Jewish people will no longer be concerned with rocket attacks from Iran, Syria, and Lebanon! A time when Jewish workers may rebuild their temple in Jerusalem. **(Rev. 11:1-3)** How come? According to Daniel, the Abomination of Desolation will defile the holy place in Jerusalem in the middle of the **70th Week**. **(Dan. 9:27, Mat. 24:15, Luke 21:20)** Which means the temple of God will be rebuilt in the first half of the **70th Week**. **(2 Thes. 2:1-4, Rev. 6:1-6)** During the Beginning of Sorrows. **(Mat. 24:4-8)**

What is this event?

'When He opened the Second Seal, I heard the second living creature saying, "Come and see." Another horse, fiery red, went out. And it was granted to the one who sat on it to take peace from the earth, and that people should kill one another...' Revelation 6:3-4

During the first half of the **70th Week**, the Lamb will open the **Second Seal** on the outside of the heavenly scroll. **(Rev. 6:3-4)** John sees a fiery red horse leave heaven. We aren't told the name of its rider. His mission is to take peace from the earth. He will achieve this by having many people kill one another. John remembered this warning from Jesus. **(Mat. 24:6)**

"And you will hear of wars and rumors of wars. See that you are not troubled; for all these things must come to pass, but the end is not yet." Matthew 24:6

After the opening of the **Second Seal (Rev. 6:3-4),** wars and rumors of wars will paralyze the nations with fear! Jesus is exhorting us not to be troubled. **(Mat. 24:6)** Because these things must come to pass before the resurrection of believers at His Coming. What things is our Lord referring to? **(Mat. 24:33)** Is it just these wars? Or should we be expecting more events before the harvest? **(Mat. 13:39)** This is an encouragement to stand firm during the painful Beginning of Sorrows. **(Mat. 24:4-8, Rev. 6:1-6)** Followed by the horrific persecution during the days of the Great Tribulation! **(Mat. 24:21-22, Dan. 12:1)** Be assured, all overcomers at His Coming will receive a crown of life! **(Rev. 2:10; 7:9-11)**

<u>Who is involved?</u>

"But he who endures to the end shall be saved." Matthew 24:13

The wicked will be terrified as wars spread around the world. We aren't told which nations are involved. Or why they're attacking each other! We aren't to be frightened by this chaos created by the rider of the red horse. **(Rev. 6:3-4)** Why not? Jesus taught John what the 'end' meant. **(Mat. 13:39)** The harvest of believers will not come until the sun, moon, and stars lose their light, the sign of the Day of The Lord. **(Isa. 13:9-11, Mat. 24:29-31, Rev. 6:12-17; 7:9-17)** Jesus has given a promise to the faithful living during the Great Tribulation. **(John 14:1-4, Mat. 24:13)** The believers overcoming the Beast and the False Prophet will be PHYSICALLY saved by the Son of Man! **(Mark 13:24-27)**

<u>When will it happen?</u>

'Then He said to them, "Nation will rise against nation, and kingdom against kingdom." Luke 21:10

The events from the first three seals Jesus calls, the Beginning of Sorrows. **(Rev. 6:1-6, Mat. 24:4-8)** The **70th Week** will begin with the opening of the **First Seal**. **(Mat. 24:4-5, Rev. 6:1-2)** It doesn't say how much time will elapse before Jesus opens the **Second Seal**. **(Mat. 24:6, Rev. 6:3-4)** The events from the **Third Seal** will complete the first half (1260 days) of this seven-year covenant. **(Mat. 24:7-8, Rev. 6:7-8)** The next day, the Abomination of Desolation will invade an unsuspecting Jerusalem. **(Mat. 24:15, Luke 21:20)** On this same day, the beginning of the Great Tribulation **(Mat. 24:21-22)**, the Lamb will open the **Fourth Seal**. **(Rev. 6:7-8)**

'And the Lord said to me, "The prophets prophesy lies in My name. I have not sent them, commanded them, nor spoken to them; they prophesy to you a false vision, divination, a worthless thing, and the deceit of their heart.' Jeremiah 14:14

We are already hearing many vainly prophesying the rider of the red horse is on the earth. They cite the wars around the world as proof. I ask you, why aren't they understanding the timing of the seven seals? **(Rev. 5:1; 6:1-17)** Sadly, the wars today can't be the wars taking place inside the future **70th Week**! This is the deceit of the hearts of prophets taking away from Daniel's prophecy! **(Jer. 14:14)**

How will it happen?

"I will go up against a land of unwalled villages; I will go to a peaceful people, who dwell safely, all of them dwelling without walls, and having neither bars nor gates." Ezekiel 38:11

The prophet Ezekiel saw the Jewish people living in peace; unprotected during the first half of the **70th Week.** **(Ezek. 38:11)** Which means the wars during the Beginning of Sorrows will not cross her borders. **(Rev. 6:3-4)** This is why the Jewish people will be unsuspecting when the Beast and his Muslim armies (horns) invade Jerusalem in the middle of the seven-year covenant. **(Mat. 24:15, Luke 21:20)**

Why will it matter?

"Watch therefore, and pray always that you may be counted worthy to escape all these things that will come to pass, and to stand before the Son of Man." Luke 21:36

Many Christians will deny their faith during the first half of the **70th Week.** **(2 Thes. 2:3-4)** Why is fellowshipping with these apostates not an option? **(Luke 21:8)** It's because anyone greeting them will share in their evil deeds. **(2 John 1:9-11)** To be clear, only the overcomers escaping Satan's wrath during the Great Tribulation will stand before the Son of Man! **(Rev. 12:12-17, Luke 21:36)**

"He who overcomes shall be clothed in white garments, and I will not blot out his name from the Book of Life; but I will confess his name before My Father and before His angels." Revelation 3:5

The overcomers will never be blotted out of the Book of Life. Instead, the Son will confess their names before His Father. **(Rev. 3:5)** My friends, may we trust in this promise no matter how much we suffer during the **70th Week**! **(Mat. 24:10-13)**

The BEGINNING OF SORROWS

The Second Seal

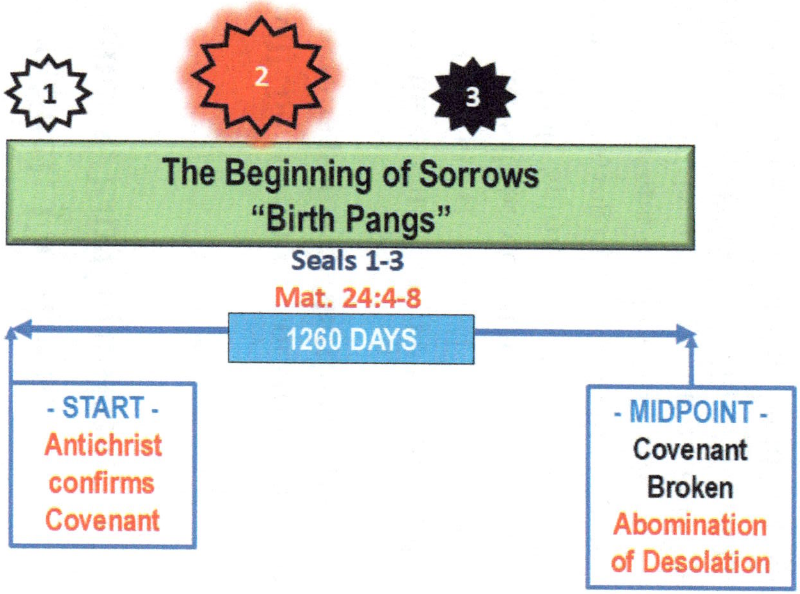

1

2

3

The Beginning of Sorrows
"Birth Pangs"

Seals 1-3

Mat. 24:4-8

1260 DAYS

- START -
Antichrist
confirms
Covenant

- MIDPOINT -
Covenant
Broken
Abomination
of Desolation

9

Third Seal: Famines, Pestilences, Earthquakes

"...And there will be famines, pestilences, and earthquakes in various places." Matthew 24:7

So far, John has seen the events from the first two seals of the heavenly scroll. **(Rev. 6:1-4)** The evil deception by the rider of the white horse will be devastating. **(Mat. 24:4-5)** Instead of obeying the Holy Spirit, many Christians will be trusting in false teachers denying the events of the Beginning of Sorrows. **(2 Pet. 2:1, Mat. 24:4-8)** They will have no idea what is coming! The brutal slaughter from the many wars after the **Second Seal** will get the attention of the wicked. Kingdom against kingdom (ethic races) will be killing each other with no end in sight. Live videos of dead bodies lying in the streets will be common. Over 5,000 religious' faiths denying the deity of Jesus will be praying for this horrific suffering to cease! Their pleading will be in vain. According to the will of God, such misery will not cease until the middle of the **70th Week**! **(Mat. 24:9-15)**

<u>What is this event?</u>

'When He opened the third seal, I heard the third living creature say, "Come and see." So, I looked, and behold, a black horse, and he who sat on it had a pair of scales in his hand.' Revelation 6:5

After the Lamb opens the **Third Seal**, John hears the third living creature say, *"Come and see."* The apostle saw a rider on a black horse. He is holding a pair of scales in his hand. A voice in the midst of the four living creatures tells him what will happen when he comes to earth. The suffering from the massive wars between the nations will be at an all-time high. The sobering reality is a daily wage won't be able to buy much food. **(Rev. 6:5)**

'And I heard a voice in the midst of the four living creatures saying, "A quart of wheat for a denarius, and three quarts of barley for a denarius; and do not harm the oil and the wine." Revelation 6:6

Jesus is warning us there will be an increase of famines after the opening of the **Third Seal** in heaven! **(Mat. 24:7-8, Rev. 6:5-6)** The voices from those starving will be crying out for a swift solution. Even so, this has a purpose. During the Beginning of Sorrows, the first three seals, Jesus will be offering salvation to a suffering world. Those willing to repent will receive forgiveness for their sins! For all refusing to believe in the gospel of our Lord Jesus Christ, Satan has other plans. The horsemen of the apocalypse will be preparing the wicked to obey the Beast and his False Prophet during the future Great Tribulation! **(Mat. 24:21-22, Rev. 13:1-18; 14:6-7)**

Who is involved?

"And there will be great earthquakes in various places, and famines and pestilences; and there will be fearful sights and great signs from heaven." Luke 21:11

There will also be great earthquakes after the opening of the **Third Seal**. The painful pestilences spreading around the world will be unimaginable. **(Luke 21:11)** At first, we won't know which nations will suffer the most! Or how many Christians will be mesmerized by the great signs from heaven. Even so, there is no evidence of a major revival during the horrors from the first three seals! Only a horrific apostasy (falling away) by believers! **(2 Thes. 2:3-4)**

When will it happen?

"When you see Jerusalem being surrounded by armies, you will know that its desolation is near." Luke 21:20

The rider of the **white horse** will arrive on earth **(Rev. 6:1-2)** the same day the Beast confirms a false peace between Jews and Muslims. **(Dan. 9:27a)** The deception by false teachers will spread like wildfire! **(Mat. 24:4-5)** The many saints blindly supporting the Beast will be obvious to the discerning. **(Rev. 13:7)** They will know the **70th Week** of Daniel prophecy is underway! **(Rev. 17:12-13)**

The rider of the **red horse** will create wars and rumors of wars in the first half of the **70th Week**. **(Rev. 6:3-4)** When we see death tolls rising among the nations, we will know this is bible prophecy. **(Mat. 24:6-7)**

The rider of the **black horse** will overwhelm the wicked with famines, earthquakes, and pestilences. **(Rev. 6:5-6)** Taking away any hope for the future will prepare the wicked to worship the Beast. So, when will this suffering end? The Beginning of Sorrows will cease in the middle of the **70th Week**. **(Mat. 24:9-15)**

The rider of the **pale horse**, Death, will come down having the power to kill one fourth of the earth. **(Rev. 6:7-8)** This same day, the Beast will break the peace he confirmed with Israel! **(Dan. 9:27, Mat. 24:15)** This invasion of Jerusalem by his armies (horns) will initiate the Great Tribulation. **(Luke 21:20, Mat. 24:21-22)** When we see the Abomination of Desolation standing in the holy place we will know the second half of the **70th Week** is underway. **(Mat. 24:15)** May we be ready to overcome by the blood of the Lamb and the word of our testimony. **(Rev. 12:11-12)**

<u>How will it happen?</u>

'And Jesus answered and said to them: "Take heed that no one deceives you." Matthew 24:4

The first three horsemen will target the rebellion by mankind in the first half of the **70th Week.** **(Mat. 24:4-8)** This is why Jesus is exhorting us not to be deceived. Anyone denying the Beginning of Sorrows is in great danger. **(Rev. 17:17)** The demonic warfare during the Great Tribulation will be much greater. **(Mat. 24:9-22)**

<u>Why will it matter?</u>

"For these are the days of vengeance, that all things which are written may be fulfilled." Luke 21:22

The day after the famines, earthquakes and pestilences cease, Jesus will open the **Fourth Seal.** **(Rev. 6:7-8)** On this same day, the Abomination of Desolation and his armies will invade an unsuspecting Jerusalem. **(Mat. 24:15, Luke 21:20)** All abiding in Christ will know how the Beast will control the world. **(Rev. 13:1-18)** The saints understanding this dark hour will be ready to overcome a persecution never seen before. **(2 Thes. 2:1-4, Dan. 12:1)** Obeying the Holy Spirit during the Beginning of Sorrows will be essential preparation for the overcomers getting the victory during the Great Tribulation. **(Luke 21:25-28, Rev. 7:9-7)** A testing of faith the Son of Man will shorten at His Coming! **(Rev. 3:10, Mat. 24:21-22, 29-31)**

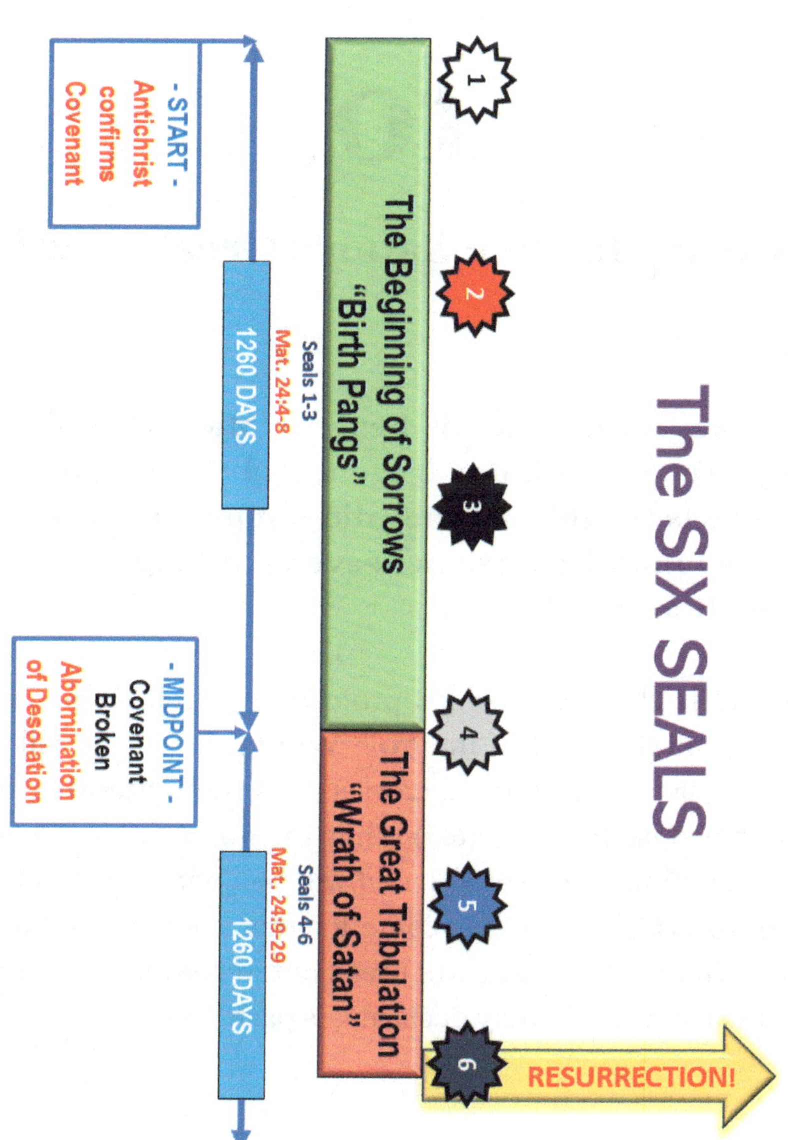
The SIX SEALS
1
2
3
4
5
6
RESURRECTION!
The Beginning of Sorrows
"Birth Pangs"
The Great Tribulation
"Wrath of Satan"
Seals 1-3
Mat. 24:4-8
1260 DAYS
Seals 4-6
Mat. 24:9-29
1260 DAYS
- START -
Antichrist
confirms
Covenant
- MIDPOINT -
Covenant
Broken
Abomination
of Desolation

10

War in Heaven: Satan's Great Wrath

'And war broke out in heaven: Michael and his angels fought with the dragon; and the dragon and his angels fought. But they did not prevail, nor was a place found for them in heaven any longer.' Revelation 12:7-8

Michael is the great prince protecting Israel. **(Dan. 12:1)** During the first half of the **70th Week**, this angel will be restraining the Mystery of Lawlessness from attacking the Jewish people. **(2 Thes. 2:6-7)** While the world suffers during the Beginning of Sorrows, Israel will be divinely protected. **(Dan. 10:21)** The time has come for this safety to be taken away. On this day, a war will break out in heaven. A conflict most teachers are falsely declaring is past. **(Rev. 12:6-17)**

What is this event?

'So the great dragon was cast out, that serpent of old, called the Devil and Satan, who deceives the whole world; he was cast to the earth, and his angels were cast out with him.' Revelation 12:9

At this moment, the accuser of the brethren is in heaven. Satan has been accusing us before God, both day and night. **(Rev. 12:10)** Yet, the Devil is aware of his eternal fate in the lake of fire! **(Rev. 20:10)** The misery from the Beginning of Sorrows has mysteriously ceased in the middle of the **70th Week**. Michael and his angels have cast the Devil and his angels out of heaven. **(Rev. 12:6-8)** Their place before the throne of God is no more. All in heaven watched as the Devil having great wrath arrives on earth. **(Rev. 12:9-12)** With Michael's restraint removed **(2 Thes. 2:7, Dan. 12:1)**, this foul spirit will persecute the Jewish people and those having the testimony of Jesus Christ. **(Rev. 12:6, 17)** Even so, the Devil already knows when the Son will cut short his time during the Great Tribulation. **(Rev. 6:12-17; 7:9-17)**

Who is involved?

'Now a great sign appeared in heaven: a woman clothed with the sun, with the moon under her feet, and on her head a garland of twelve stars...Then the woman fled into the wilderness, where she has a place prepared by God, that they should feed her there one thousand two hundred and sixty days.' Revelation 12:1, 6

Michael, the restrainer, has been taken out of the way. **(Dan. 12:1, 2 Thes. 2:7)** Satan has come down to earth having great wrath! So who will he attack first? The Woman represents Jewish survivors from the first half of the **70th Week**. **(Rev. 12:6)** Satan will try persecuting the people who gave birth to the Christ child! **(Rev. 12:13-14)** How will our Lord intervene? This remnant will flee into the wilderness. **(Mat. 24:15-20)** They will arrive safely to a place prepared by God. **(Rev. 12:6)** The Woman will be protected from the presence of Satan for the entire second half of the **70th Week** (1260 days). **(Rev. 12:14)** The dragon will become enraged. Unable to reach her, Satan will war against all having the testimony of Jesus! **(Rev. 12:17)**

'For I will take you from among the nations, gather you out of all countries, and bring you into your own land.' Ezekiel 36:24

The Lord has already brought millions of Jews back to their homeland in unbelief. **(Ezek. 36:20-24, Mat. 23:37-39)** In his vision, John saw twelve stars on the head of the Woman. **(Rev. 12:1)** These stars represent 144,000 men from the twelve tribes of Israel. **(Rev. 7:1-8)** After the 70th Week ends, the Christ will physically gather them from the wilderness! **(Isa. 63:1-6, Rev. 12:6; 14:1-4)**

"For I do not desire, brethren, that you should be ignorant of this mystery, lest you should be wise in your own opinion, that blindness in part has happened to Israel until the fullness of the Gentiles has come in...For this is My covenant with them, When I take away their sins." Romans 11:25, 27

The resurrection of believers from heaven and earth will initiate His Second Coming. **(Mark 13:24-27, Rev. 7:9-17)** Jesus and Paul each taught this gathering will take place during the Feast of Trumpets. **(Mat. 24:36, Mark 13:24-27, 1 Thes. 4:15-17)** Paul also shared the future salvation of Israel. **(Heb. 9:28)** This is why he warned Gentile believers not to be ignorant concerning the Jew's blindness to the gospel. **(Rom. 11:25-27)** When the fullness of the **70th Week** ends, the Christ will complete the mystery of God. **(Rev. 10:1-7)** The Most Holy will turn away ungodliness from Jacob and forgive one third of Israel on the Day of Atonement. **(Dan. 9:24, Zech. 13:8-9)** Anyone denying the fulfillment of these Feasts of The Lord is taking away from the Second Coming of Christ! **(Rev. 22:19)**

<u>**When will it happen?**</u>

'Then I heard a loud voice saying in heaven, "Now salvation, and strength, and the kingdom of our God, and the power of His Christ have come, for the accuser of our brethren, who accused them before our God day and night, has been cast down.' Revelation 12:10

The war between Michael and Satan will begin the second half of the **70th Week** (1260 days). **(Rev. 12:6-12)** During this heavenly conflict, the salvation and strength of the kingdom of our God will come! A loud voice will announce the Devil has been cast out of heaven for good! **(Rev. 12:10)** Only by the power of Christ will the accuser of the brethren be cast down to earth. The discerning believers seeing a remnant of Jews fleeing into the wilderness will know why. **(Mat. 24:15-16, Rev. 12:6-12)** The Abomination of Desolation is standing in the temple of God (**Mat. 24:15, 2 Thes. 2:3-4)** and Michael the restrainer has been taken out of the way. **(2 Thes. 2:7, Dan. 12:1; 10:21)**

<u>How will it happen?</u>

"At that time Michael shall stand up, the great prince who stands watch over the sons of your people; And there shall be a time of trouble, Such as never was since there was a nation, Even to that time. And at that time your people shall be delivered, Every one who is found written in the book." Daniel 12:1

The Great Tribulation will begin the same day Michael casts Satan down to earth. **(Rev. 12:7-12)** Yet, most pastors are teaching the restrainer is somehow the Holy Spirit! Why is this so dangerous? It's because there will be people receiving the Holy Spirit during the Great Tribulation **(Rev. 12:17)**, during the Day of The Lord **(Rev. 10:7)**, even during the 1,000 year reign of Christ. **(Rev. 21:9-10, 24)** The Holy Spirit will never be taken away, not in this age nor in the age to come. **(Mat. 12:32)**

'And the Spirit and the bride say, "Come!" And let him who hears say, "Come!" And let him who thirsts come. Whoever desires, let him take the water of life freely.' Revelation 22:17

There are others believing the church is the restrainer. The truth is, Satan will be cast down to earth by Michael the same day the Lamb opens the **Fourth Seal**. **(Rev. 6:7-8; 12:9-12)** The church won't be caught up out of the Great Tribulation till after the opening of the **Sixth Seal**! **(Rev. 6:12-17; 7:9-17)**

<u>Why will it matter?</u>

'And the dragon was enraged with the woman, and he went to make war with the rest of her offspring, who keep the commandments of God and have the testimony of Jesus Christ.' Revelation 12:17

The dragon doesn't want anyone to understand the timing of the Great Tribulation. **(Mat. 24:15, 21-22, 29)** When the Devil arrives having great wrath, the world will worship him and the Beast. **(Rev. 12:12-17; 13:4-5)** The wicked living in peace and safety will have no idea their destruction is coming. **(1 Thes. 5:3, Mat. 24:37-39)** To be clear, only those overcoming during the Great Tribulation **(Rev. 7:9-17)** will be physically saved by angels at the Coming of The Son of Man. **(Mark 13:24-27)**

'But I will tell you what is noted in the Scripture of Truth. No one upholds me against these, except Michael your prince.' Daniel 10:21

Michael the prince is currently protecting the children of Israel. **(Dan. 10:21)** Until a great trouble never seen before comes upon them. **(Dan. 12:1)** During Jacobs Trouble, the Great Tribulation, who will have the love and courage to give their life for the sake of Christ? **(Mat. 24:9-12, 21-22)**

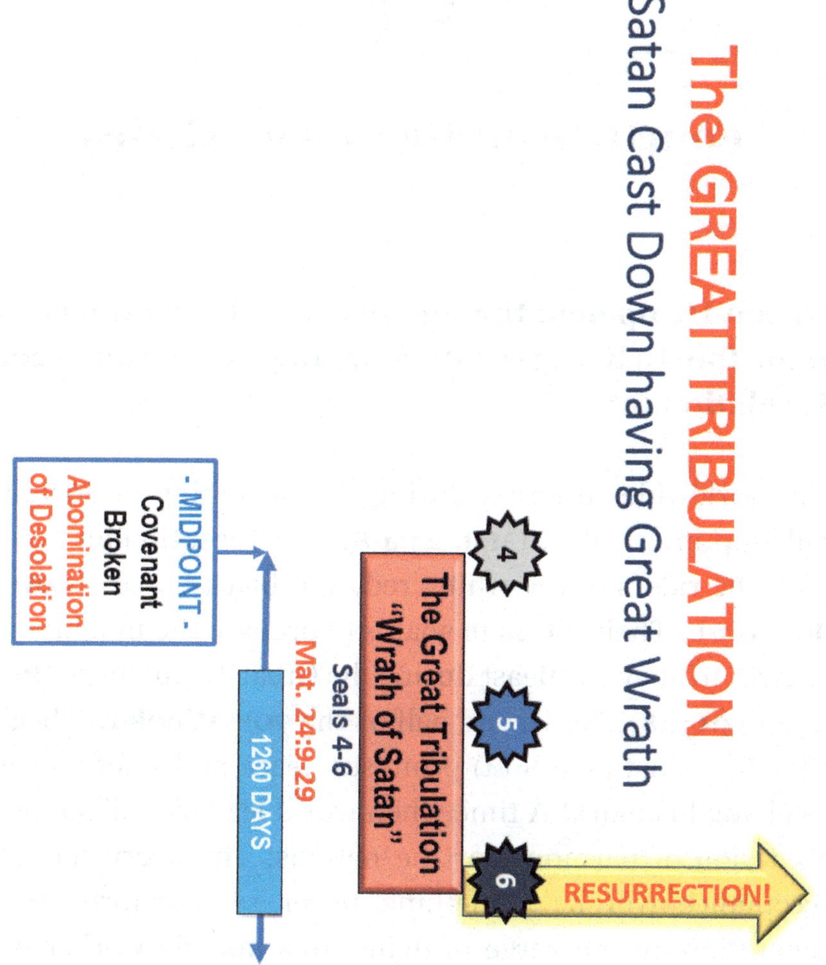
The GREAT TRIBULATION
Satan Cast Down having Great Wrath
RESURRECTION!
4
5
6
The Great Tribulation
"Wrath of Satan"
Seals 4-6
Mat. 24:9-29
1260 DAYS
- MIDPOINT -
Covenant
Broken
Abomination
of Desolation

11

Fourth Seal: Death and Hades

"When He opened the fourth seal, I heard the voice of the fourth living creature saying, "Come and see." Revelation 6:7

The worldwide suffering during the Beginning of Sorrows will stop in one day. **(Mat. 24:4-8)** The deception and pain from the riders of the white, red, and black horses is over. **(Rev. 6:1-6)** Their ultimate goal is to prepare the inhabitants of earth to obey the Beast during the Great Tribulation. **(Rev. 12:12; 13:15-18)** The second half of the **70th Week** will begin after the Beast (Antichrist) promises peace and safety for all receiving his mark! A time when world leaders will support his vision of harmony for the nations. The overwhelming acceptance will be something never seen before. To a generation on the verge of dying, this miracle worker will offer a hope for the future! A lie from the very lips of the enemy! **(Rev. 14:9-11)**

'...The dragon gave him his power, his throne, and great authority.' Revelation 13:2b

Michael has cast Satan down to earth having great wrath. **(Rev. 12:12)** This angel is no longer restraining the children of Israel from the Mystery of Lawlessness. **(Dan. 12:1, 2 Thes. 2:7)** Satan will begin by persecuting the Jewish people. **(Mat. 24:15-20)** One third will respond by fleeing to a place of safety prepared by God. **(Zech. 13:9, Rev. 12:6, 14)** Enraged, Satan will turn away and make war against those having the testimony of Jesus! **(Rev. 12:17)** During the Great Tribulation, this foul spirit will do something never seen before! The dragon (Satan) will give the Beast His power, his throne, and great authority over the nations. **(Rev. 13:2b)**

<u>What is this event?</u>

'When He opened the fourth seal, I heard the voice of the fourth living creature saying, "Come and see. So I looked, and behold, a pale horse. And the name of him who sat on it was Death, and Hades followed with him...' Revelation 6:8

After the opening of the **Fourth Seal**, John sees a pale horse in heaven. Its rider is called Death. And Hades is following him. **(Rev. 6:7-8)** Their evil mission is clear. They will create a time of trouble never seen before! **(Dan. 12:1, Mat. 24:21-22)** They will arrive on earth, with the power to kill one fourth of mankind. This marks the beginning of the Great Tribulation against those having the testimony of Jesus. **(Rev. 12:12, 17)**

A critical revelation rarely taught. Instead, we often hear, *"The church will be caught up before the Great Tribulation begins!"* I challenge you; the above deception is not biblical nor from the Spirit of God. **(Rev. 7:9-17)**

"Therefore when you see the 'abomination of desolation,' spoken of by Daniel the prophet, standing in the holy place" (whoever reads, let him understand)." Matthew 24:15

Jesus revealed to John when the Great Tribulation will begin. **(Mat. 24:21-22)** The Lamb will open the **Fourth Seal** the same day the Man of Sin exalts himself in the temple of God in Jerusalem. **(2 Thes. 2:3-4, Mat. 24:9-15, Rev. 6:7-8)** This is not blind faith. Anyone refusing to take the mark of the Beast will be targeted by the False Prophet. **(Rev. 13:11-18)** This is why Jesus has promised to shorten (amputate) the Great Tribulation by His Second Coming. **(Mat. 24:21-22, 29-31, Mark 13:24-27)**

'... And power was given to them over a fourth of the earth, to kill with sword, with hunger, with death, and by the beasts of the earth.' Revelation 6:8

In The Revelation of Jesus Christ, 'beast' is used thirty-two times. **(Rev. 13:1; 14:11; 15:2; 17:13)** Beast never refers to animals in this letter. Death and Hades will kill through the two beasts. **(Rev. 13:1-18)** The Beast and the False Prophet will have the power to kill over a fourth of the earth during the Great Tribulation. **(Rev. 6:8)**

'Then I saw another beast coming up out of the earth, and he had two horns like a lamb and spoke like a dragon. And he exercises all the authority of the first beast in his presence, and causes the earth and those who dwell in it to worship the first beast...' Revelation 13:11-12

The second beast will exercise the power of the first beast while in his presence. The False Prophet will look like a lamb but speak like a dragon. **(Rev. 13:11-12)** The day the Abomination of Desolation surrounds Jerusalem **(Mat. 24:15, Luke 21:20)**, the False Prophet will convince the inhabitants of earth to worship him. A time when the unrighteous will prosper, while the righteous suffer. **(Rev. 12:12; 13:4)**

'He causes all, both small and great, rich and poor, free and slave, to receive a mark on their right hand or on their foreheads, and that no one may buy or sell except one who has the mark or the name of the beast, or the number of his name.'
Revelation 13:16-17

The Great Tribulation will begin the day the Beast announces his edict! Everyone must receive his mark on their right hand or forehead. **(Rev. 13:16-17)** The faithful refusing will face unprecedented persecution. **(Dan. 12:1, Mat. 24:21-22)** And what will happen to believers overcoming Satan's great wrath by the blood of the Lamb? **(Rev. 12:11-12)** For those who do, there is a heavenly reward! **(Rev. 3:5)**

Who is involved?

"For then there will be great tribulation, such as has not been since the beginning of the world until this time, no, nor ever shall be." Matthew 24:21

According to Jesus, these three time periods will take place during the future **70th Week** of Daniel. **(Dan. 9:24-27, Matthew 24:3-33)**

(1) The rebellion by man during the **Beginning of Sorrows** will last 3 1/2 years (1260 days). The entire first half of the **70th Week. (Mat. 24:4-8)** This prophecy will begin with the opening of the **First Seal. (Rev. 6:1-2)** The first half will end the day the suffering from the **Third Seal** ceases. **(Rev. 6:1-6)**

(2) Satan's great wrath during the **Great Tribulation** will begin the second half of the **70th Week**. **(Rev. 12:12, Mat. 24:15-22)** This demonic persecution will take place during the **Fourth and Fifth Seals**. **(Rev. 6:7-11)** The Great Tribulation will be cut short the day the Lamb opens the **Sixth Seal**. **(Mat. 24:29, Rev. 6:7-11; 7:9-17)**

(3) The wrath of the Lamb will begin destroying sinners after the constellations lose their light! **(Mat. 24:29, Rev. 6:12-17)** On this same day, the beginning of **The Day of the Lord (Isa. 13:9-11)**, every eye will see the sign of the Son of Man. **(Rev. 1:7, Mat. 24:30)** Jesus is coming back in the glory of His Father! **(Mat. 16:27)**

"Then they will deliver you up to tribulation and kill you, and you will be hated by all nations for My name's sake.' Matthew 24:9

During the Great Tribulation all refusing to obey the Beast for the sake of Christ will be considered a threat. **(Rev. 13:11-18)** The nations will hate Christians, delivering them up to be killed! **(Mat. 24:9-14)** Even so, a great multitude of overcomers will be watching for the sign of the Day of The Lord. **(Isa. 13:9-11, Mat. 24:29, Mark 13:24-27)** A time of darkness when Jesus will send forth angels to physically save them out of the Great Tribulation! **(Rev. 7:9-17)**

'You will say, 'I will go up against a land of unwalled villages; I will go to a peaceful people, who dwell safely, all of them dwelling without walls, and having neither bars nor gates.' Ezekiel 38:11

After confirming a peace with Israel **(Dan. 9:27b)**, why will the world treat the Beast like a savior? **(Rev. 13:3-4)** Due to this controversial covenant, Israel will be protected from her enemies in the first half of the **70th Week. (Ezek. 38:11)**

While the nations suffer the misery from the Beginning of Sorrows. **(Mat. 24:4-8)** And when will the Great Tribulation begin the second half of this seven year covenant? The very day the Abomination of Desolation and his armies surround an unsuspecting people living in Jerusalem! **(Mat. 24:15, Luke 21:20)**

'And he deceives those who dwell on the earth by those signs which he was granted to do in the sight of the beast, telling those who dwell on the earth to make an image to the beast who was wounded by the sword and lived.' Revelation 13:12-13

Why will the wicked be living in peace and safety during the Great Tribulation? **(1 Thes. 5:3)** While in the presence of the Beast, the False Prophet will deceive those dwelling on the earth by performing great signs. **(Rev. 13:12-13)** Anyone refusing to obey, the second beast will hunt down and kill. **(Rev. 13:11-18)**

"And I will give, power to my two witnesses, and they will prophesy one thousand two hundred and sixty days, clothed in sackcloth." Revelation 11:3

The same day the Great Tribulation begins **(Mat. 24:15)**, two prophets will arrive in Jerusalem. **(Rev. 11:2-6)** John calls them the Two Witnesses. God will give them the power to prophesy the entire second half of the **70th Week** (1,260 days). The same time the Beast will have power over the nations (1,260 days). **(Rev. 13:5)** Considering the timing of their arrival, the Two Witnesses may begin by exposing the evil agenda of the Beast. **(Rev. 13:5-7)** After declaring the Great Tribulation is underway, they may prophesy the resurrection of believers by the Son of Man will precede the Day of The Lord, the wrath of the Lamb! **(Mat. 24:21-31, 37-39, Rev. 7:9-17; 8:1-5)** And no one will stop these prophets from declaring the physical return of Christ at the end of the **70th Week.** **(Dan. 9:24, Heb. 9:28, Rom. 11:25-27, Rev. 10:7)**

When will it happen?

'And I saw three unclean spirits like frogs coming out of the mouth of the dragon, out of the mouth of the beast, and out of the mouth of the false prophet.' Revelation 16:13

During the days of the Great Tribulation **(Rev. 13:1-18)**, three unclean spirits will come out of the mouths of the Dragon, the Beast, and the False Prophet. **(Rev. 16:13)** They will form an unholy trinity against the saints of God. **(Rev. 12:17; 13:7)** Even so, they will know the days of their wrath are numbered. **(Rev. 7:9-17)**

'So they worshiped the dragon who gave authority to the beast; and they worshiped the beast, saying, "Who is like the beast? Who is able to make war with him?" Revelation 13:4

The suffering from the Beginning of Sorrows is over. **(Mat. 24:8)** All the world will marvel. **(Rev. 13:3-4)** The pompous Beast will take credit for this so-called miracle. So when will the world worship Satan and the Beast? Their blasphemy will begin the second half of the **70th Week**. **(Rev. 13:5, 2 Thes. 2:3-4)** Billions lining up to take his mark will look like a great celebration. **(Rev. 13:12-14)** Most will trust him to usher in a unity never seen before. In response, God will send three angels.

'Then I saw another angel flying in the midst of heaven, having the everlasting gospel to preach to those who dwell on the earth—to every nation, tribe, tongue, and people—saying with a loud voice, "Fear God and give glory to Him, for the hour of His judgment has come; and worship Him who made heaven and earth, the sea and springs of water." Revelation 14:6-7

(1) John saw an angel flying in the midst of heaven. **(Rev. 14:6-7)** He is coming down to preach the everlasting gospel to everyone on earth. This is the fulfillment of the prophecy Jesus promised. **(Mark 13:10)** During the Great Tribulation, the gospel of the kingdom will be preached in all the world. **(Mat. 24:14-22, Rev. 7:9-17)** Everyone will have the opportunity to be physically saved by the Son of Man before the wrath of the Lamb is unleashed on this Christ rejecting world. **(Luke 17:30, Rev. 6:16-17)**

‘And another angel followed, saying, “Babylon is fallen, is fallen, that great city, because she has made all nations drink of the wine of the wrath of her fornication.” Revelation 14:8

(2) On the first day of the Great Tribulation, a second angel will announce the fall of Babylon, the mother of all harlots. Since her inception, Mystery Babylon has made the nations drink the wine of her fornication. **(Rev. 17:1-5)** Her harlots, all religious faiths denying Jesus, will choose to worship the Beast and receive his mark. The final judgment of this religious counterfeit has finally come. **(Rev. 14:8)**

‘...“If anyone worships the beast and his image, and receives his mark on his forehead or on his hand, he himself shall also drink of the wine of the wrath of God, which is poured out full strength into the cup of His indignation. He shall be tormented with fire and brimstone in the presence of the holy angels and in the presence of the Lamb.”
Revelation 14:9-10

(3) A third angel will warn all living on the first day of the Great Tribulation. **(Rev. 13:1-18; 14:9-11)** Anyone choosing to worship the Beast, his image, and receive his mark will be tormented with fire and brimstone in the presence of the Lamb! The smoke of their torment will ascend forever and ever! **(Rev. 20:11-15)**

"But when you see Jerusalem surrounded by armies, then know that its desolation is near." Luke 21:20

On the same day, the armies of the Beast will surround an unsuspecting Jerusalem. **(Luke 21:20)** His blasphemy within the temple of God will mean nothing to the wicked. **(2 Thes. 2:3-4, Rev. 13:2-6)** At first, many leaders will renounce such betrayal. After hearing his guarantee of peace, their distain will suddenly change. With support from the popular False Prophet, the acceptance of the Beast will be a done deal. This same day, the Lamb will open the **Fourth Seal. (Rev. 6:7-8)**

"So when you see the 'abomination of desolation,' spoken of by Daniel the prophet, standing where it ought not" (let the reader understand), "then let those who are in Judea flee to the mountains. Let him who is on the housetop not go down into the house, nor enter to take anything out of his house." Mark 13:13-15

The second half of the **70th Week** will also be a day of reckoning for unsaved Israel. **(Mat. 24:15)** For those living in Judea, Jesus has told them what to do. **(Rev. 12:6)** Their betrayal will be clear after seeing the Abomination of Desolation standing in the temple of God. **(Mark 13:13-15)** They will have one option. They must flee to the mountains. Zechariah tells us the fate of those that don't make it. Two thirds will die by the end of the **70th Week. (Zech. 13:8-9)**

‘For when they say, “Peace and safety!” then sudden destruction comes upon them, as labor pains upon a pregnant woman. And they shall not escape.’ 1 Thessalonians 5:3

When will the wicked be living in peace and safety during the **70th Week?** **(1 Thes. 5:3)** Will it be during the Beginning of Sorrows, the Great Tribulation, or The Day of The Lord? During the Beginning of Sorrows, the wicked will suffer from wars, famines, earthquakes, and pestilences! **(Mat. 24:4-8)** No one suffering such misery will be living in peace and safety. During the Day of The Lord, Jesus will punish the wicked with wrath and fierce anger. **(Isa. 13:9-11)** The torment during the trumpet judgments will be beyond belief. Clearly, the followers of the Beast won’t be living in peace and safety during the wrath of the Lamb. **(Rev. 6:16-17; 8:1-2)**

‘Looking for the blessed hope and glorious appearing of our great God and Savior Jesus Christ.’ Titus 2:13

The only time the wicked will be enjoying peace and safety is during the Great Tribulation. **(Mat. 24:21-22, 25)** Like in the days of Noah, the followers of the Beast will be eating, drinking, and getting married. **(Mat. 24:37-39)** Only the overcomers will understand the consequences of this dark hour. **(Titus 2:12-13, Rev. 7:9-17)**

How will it happen?

"Watch therefore, and pray always that you may be counted worthy to escape all these things that will come to pass, and to stand before the Son of Man." Luke 21:36

How will Christians escape Satan's wrath during the Great Tribulation? **(Rev. 12:11-12)** The resurrection will cut short this persecution AFTER the opening of the **Sixth Seal**. **(Rev. 6:12-17; 7:9-17)** This same day the wrath of the Lamb will begin destroying sinners. **(Isa. 13:9-11)** So why is Satan hiding this truth? It's because only those overcoming the Beast and the False Prophet will stand before the Son of Man! **(Rev. 13:1-18, Luke 21:24-36)**

'For God did not appoint us to wrath, but to obtain salvation through our Lord Jesus Christ.'
1 Thessalonians 5:9

The suffering during the Beginning of Sorrows will end the day the Lamb opens the **Fourth Seal**. **(Rev. 6:7-8)** It will be a massive relief for the wicked worshiping the Beast during the Great Tribulation. **(Rev. 13:2-5)** They will ignore the warning by the third angel not to take his mark. **(Rev. 14:9-10)** The faithful will be caught up to heaven the day the Lamb opens the **Sixth Seal. (Rev. 7:9-17)** That same day the followers of the Beast will suffer the wrath of the Lamb! **(1 Thes. 5:9, Isa. 13:9-11)**

Why will it matter?

'Looking for the blessed hope and glorious appearing of our great God and Savior Jesus Christ.' Titus 2:13

Our great God and Savior Jesus is our Blessed Hope. **(Titus 2:13)** Most have been taught they will lose their Blessed Hope if they're persecuted by the Beast. **(Rev. 13:5-7)** Actually, His promise to deliver believers out of the Great Tribulation produces hope. **(Mat. 24:21-22)** The empowering to overcome does not take away our Blessed Hope; it enhances it. **(Rev. 3:5; 7:9-17; 12:11)**

'…"These are the ones who come out of the great tribulation, and washed their robes and made them white in the blood of the Lamb." Revelation 7:14b

"My pastor really understands the end times. When he teaches the church won't be here for the Great Tribulation, I can just feel the Holy Spirit!" (False)

Cloaked in darkness, a great multitude of blood washed overcomers will come out of the Great Tribulation and stand before the Father and the Lamb! **(Rev. 7:9-17)** This is the only time the Son will come back in the glory of His Father and gather His elect to heaven. The same day He will pour out His wrath on the wicked left behind. **(Mat. 16:27, Mark 13:24-27, Mat. 24:29-31, 37-39)**

"But in those days, after that tribulation, the sun will be darkened, and the moon will not give its light; the stars of heaven will fall, and the powers in the heavens will be shaken. Then they will see the Son of Man coming in the clouds with great power and glory." Mark 13:24-26

"No one knows when the Son will come back for us. It's just a bunch of guesswork. Anyone who claims to know is a liar." (False)

Jesus has already told us the day He will gather a great multitude of believers out of the Great Tribulation. **(Mat. 24:21-22, Rev. 7:9-17)** It's called the sign of the Day of The Lord. **(Isa. 13:9-11)** The very day the sun, moon, and stars lose their light during the Feast of Trumpets **(Mat. 24:29-36)** every eye will see the Son coming in the clouds with great power and glory. **(Rev. 1:7, Mat. 16:27, Mark 13:24-27)**

"Blessed is he who reads and those who hear the words of this prophecy, and keep those things which are written in it; for the time is near." Revelation 1:3

Many ask, *"Why is The Book of Revelation so confusing? How can I keep the things in this prophecy if I don't understand them?"*

My friends, understanding the meaning of every verse and symbol in The Revelation of Jesus Christ is not our goal.

There is a reason why this prophetic letter is hard to understand! Simply, the events John wrote down are not in chronological order. If you ask the Holy Spirit, He will teach you the events taking place before, during and after the Second Coming of Christ. **(Rev. 1:1-3)**

'But you, brethren, are not in darkness, so that this Day should overtake you as a thief. You are all sons of light and sons of the day. We are not of the night nor of darkness.' 1 Thessalonians 5:4-5

For example, we have just studied the events which will take place between the **Third** and **Fourth Seals**. **(Rev. 6:5-6, 7-8)** Yet, these events will take place on the same day! Let's review them to understand their timing and their consequences.

"...Now salvation, and strength, and the kingdom of our God, and the power of His Christ have come, for the accuser of our brethren, who accused them before our God day and night, has been cast down." Revelation 12:10

On the first day of the second half of the **70th Week**, Satan will be in heaven accusing believers before God. On this same day, the archangel Michael and his angels will war against the dragon and his angels. **(Rev. 12:7-11)**

On this same day, Michael will cast the accuser of the brethren down to earth. **(Rev. 12:9)** Immediately, the restrainer will stand aside! **(Dan. 12:1; 10:21)** Michael will no longer restrain the Mystery of Lawlessness from attacking Israel. **(2 Thes. 2:6-7)**

On this same day, the Devil will come down to earth having great wrath. **(Rev. 12:12)** He knows when his time to deceive during the Great Tribulation will end. **(Rev. 6:12-17)** He will begin by trying to persecute the Woman, the Jewish people. **(Rev. 12:6)** On this same day, a remnant of Jews will flee into the wilderness to a place prepared by God. The Woman will be protected from the presence of Satan for the second half of the **70th Week**. **(Rev. 12:13-14)**

On this same day, an enraged Satan will then make war against those having the testimony of Jesus. **(Rev. 12:17)** The Devil will begin by giving the Beast his power over the nations for the second half of the **70th Week**. **(Rev. 13:1-5)**

On this same day, the Abomination of Desolation will break the peace he brokered with Israel. **(Mat. 24:15)** The armies from his ten nations (horns) will surround an unsuspecting Jerusalem. **(Dan. 7:20, Rev. 17:12-13, Luke 21:20)** The world will watch as the Man of Sin (Antichrist) exalts himself in the temple of God. **(2 Thes. 2:3-4)**

On this same day, the Two Witnesses will begin prophesying. **(Rev. 11:3)** The same time the world is worshiping the Beast. **(Rev. 13:4)** These two prophets will actually hear him blaspheme God, His tabernacle, and those dwelling in heaven. **(Rev. 13:6)**

On this same day, three angels will arrive. The first angel will preach the everlasting gospel to everyone on earth. **(Rev. 14:6-7)** The second angel will announce the fall of Babylon, the mother of all harlots. **(Rev. 14:8)** The third angel will warn everyone not to worship the Beast, his image, nor receive his mark. **(Rev. 14:9-11)**

'It was granted to him to make war with the saints and to overcome them. And authority was given him over every tribe, tongue, and nation.'
Revelation 13:7

On this same day, the Lamb will open the **Fourth Seal**. **(Rev. 6:7-8)** The rider of the pale horse, Death, will come down to earth! There is no way of knowing how many saints the Beast will overcome during the Great Tribulation. **(Rev. 13:5-7)**

The First Day of The Great Tribulation

1. Satan having great wrath will be cast down to earth.
2. Michael the restrainer will be taken out of the way.
3. A remnant of Jews will be protected for 1,260 days.
4. The Beast is given power over the nations for 1,260 days.
5. Two Witnesses will prophesy for 1,260 days.
6. The Abomination of Desolation will invade Jerusalem.
7. The first angel will preach the gospel to every nation.
8. The second angel will announce the fall of Babylon.
9. The third angel will warn not to worship the Beast.
10. The Fourth Seal will be opened in heaven.

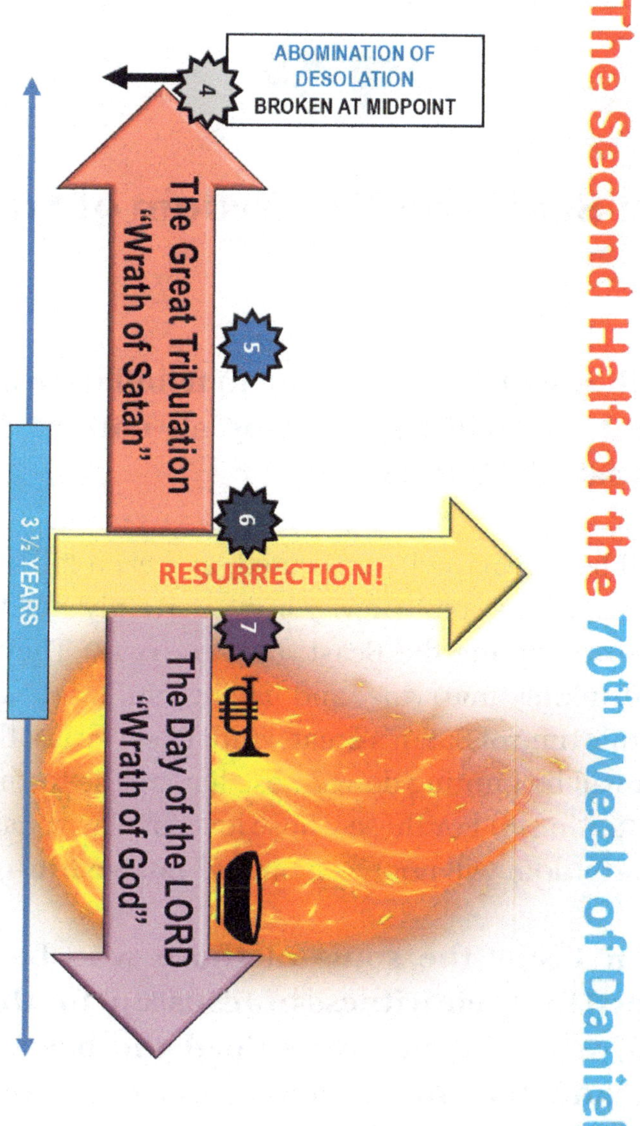
The Second Half of the 70th Week of Daniel
ABOMINATION OF DESOLATION
BROKEN AT MIDPOINT
4
The Great Tribulation
"Wrath of Satan"
5
6
RESURRECTION!
7
The Day of the LORD
"Wrath of God"
3 ½ YEARS

12

Fifth Seal: The Martyrdom of Saints

"Then they will deliver you up to tribulation and kill you, and you will be hated by all nations for My name's sake." Matthew 24:9

Who will be threatened, persecuted, and even killed during the Great Tribulation? **(Rev. 7:9-17)** Certainly not the vast majority worshiping the Beast! **(Rev. 13:11-18)** They will be eating, drinking, marrying, and having fun. **(Mat. 24:37-39)** During this time of Satan's great wrath **(Rev. 12:12)**, the False Prophet will be hunting down those having the testimony of Jesus! **(Rev. 12:17)** For those whose love for Christ has grown cold, martyrdom will not be an option! **(Mat. 24:10-13)**

'... Then I saw the souls of those who had been beheaded for their witness to Jesus and for the word of God, who had not worshiped the beast or his image, and had not received his mark on their foreheads or on their hands...' Revelation 20:4

The **Fourth Seal** on the outside of the heavenly scroll lay open. **(Rev. 6:7-8)** The rider of the pale horse, Death, has the power to kill over a fourth of the world by the two beasts. **(Rev. 13:1-18)** During the Great Tribulation, the Beast and his False Prophet will control the nations by the power of Satan. **(Rev. 12:7-14; 13:1-18)** For the safety of their members, over 5,000 religious faiths will choose to comply. Almost overnight a resistance movement will rise up. The False Prophet will announce such evil has to be eliminated. All breaking the law by refusing to worship the Beast will receive the death penalty. We don't know how many officers will be sent out to capture the faithful believers resisting. **(Rev. 13:15-16; 14:9-11)**

"Therefore whoever confesses Me before men, him I will also confess before My Father who is in heaven. But whoever denies Me before men, him I will also deny before My Father who is in heaven." Matthew 10:32-33

During the Great Tribulation, the nations will hate Christians. **(Mat. 24:9-22)** Those no longer abiding in Christ will be overcome by the Beast. **(2 John 1:9-11, Rev. 13:7)** To avoid persecution, even martyrdom, a son will betray his father, a daughter will betray her mother. **(Mat. 10:32-37)** How so? By reporting them to the False Prophet! **(Rev. 13:11-18)** A time when overcomers will love the Lord more than their own family!

What is this event?

'When He opened the fifth seal, I saw under the altar the souls of those who had been slain for the word of God and for the testimony which they held.' Revelation 6:9

After the **Fifth Seal**, John saw souls under the altar in heaven. **(Rev. 6:9-11)** These are the martyrs from the Great Tribulation. **(Rev. 6:7-8; 20:4)** Rather than deny their Lord, they will overcome by the word of God and their testimony. **(Rev. 6:9)** This why so many will ignore the warning not to be deceived! **(Mat. 24:4-5)**

'It was granted to him to make war with the saints and to overcome them. And authority was given him over every tongue and nation.' Revelation 13:7

What saints will the Beast overcome? **(Rev. 13:7)** Many during the Great Tribulation will ignore the warning by the third angel. **(Rev. 14:9-11)** Instead, they will believe there is no sin God can't forgive. The result, many will ask God for forgiveness after worshiping the Beast. This will never happen. Mercy will no longer be available to Christians having his mark, 666. **(Rev. 13:11-18)** During the supper of the great God, Jesus will kill every follower of the Beast. None will survive the great day of God Almighty, Armageddon. **(Rev. 13:16; 16:14-16; 19:20-21)**

Who is involved?

'And they cried with a loud voice, saying, "How long, O Lord, holy and true, until You judge and avenge our blood on those who dwell on the earth?" Revelation 6:10

There will be many killed for their faith during the Great Tribulation. **(Rev. 13:11-18; 20:4)** John saw these martyrs under the altar in heaven. They're asking how long it will be before God avenges those who shed their blood? **(Rev. 6:9-11)**

'Alas! For that day is great, so that none is like it; And it is the time of Jacob's trouble, but he shall be saved out of it.' Jeremiah 30:7

Many are convinced Jesus will never allow His future bride to suffer during the **70th Week**. **(Rev. 13:15)** They believe this seven year covenant is only for unsaved Israel! Yet, many Christians will depart from the faith during the Great Tribulation. **(2 Thes. 2:3-4)** This is why both will be tested during the Great Tribulation, also called Jacob's Trouble! **(Mat. 24:21-22, Jer. 30:7)**

'The coming of the lawless one is according to the working of Satan, with all power, signs, and lying wonders, and with all unrighteous deception among those who perish, because they did not receive the love of the truth, that they might be saved. And for this reason God will send them strong delusion, that they should believe the lie.' 2 Thessalonians 2:9-11

The coming of the lawless one, the Beast, will deceive by the power of Satan. **(Rev. 13:3-4)** The wicked will trust in his false signs and lying wonders. Complemented by the miracles the False Prophet will perform while in his presence! **(Rev. 13:13-14)** So what will happen to the saints refusing the love of the truth during the Great Tribulation? **(Rev. 13:7)** All having the mark of the Beast will receive a strong delusion from God. **(2 Thes. 2:9-11)** They will eventually be tormented with the cup of His indignation. **(Rev. 14:10)**

<u>When will it happen?</u>

"When they finish their testimony, the beast that ascends out of the bottomless pit will make war against them, overcome them, and kill them." Revelation 11:7

The Lamb will open the **First, Second** and **Third Seals** in the first half of the **70th Week. (Rev. 6:1-6)** Our Lord will open the **Fourth, Fifth, Sixth**, and **Seventh Seals** in the second half. **(Rev. 6:7-17; 8:1)** The Great Tribulation will begin the day Jesus opens the **Fourth Seal**. **(Mat. 24:15-22, Rev. 6:7-8)** John saw the believers martyred by the two beasts after the opening of the **Fifth Seal**. **(Rev. 6:9-11, Rev. 20:4)** Every eye will see the resurrection of overcomers after the opening of the **Sixth Seal. (Rev. 6:12-17; 7:9-17)** On the same day, the wrath of the Lamb will begin destroying sinners after the opening of the **Seventh Seal. (Isa. 13:9-11, 8:1-5)** The day after the **70th Week** ends, the Beast will kill the Two Witnesses between the **Sixth** and **Seventh Trumpets**.

(Rev. 9:13; 11:7-8, 15) Which proves the Lamb will open all **Seven Seals** during the **70th Week.** **(Rev. 6:1-17; 8:1)**

"And then many will be offended, will betray one another, and will hate one another. Then many false prophets will rise up and deceive many. And because lawlessness will abound, the love of many will grow cold. But he who endures to the end shall be saved. Matthew 24:10-13

Jesus, Paul, and John each prophesied of this dark time. **(Mat. 24:10-13, 2 Thes. 2:3-4, Rev. 12:6-17)** Satan's wrath after the **Fourth** and **Fifth Seals** will be the worst persecution in history! **(Dan. 12:1, Rev. 12:12, 17)** The pathetic refusal by the wicked to believe the gospel angel will be heartbreaking. **(Rev. 14:6-7)** Instead of a great revival, we may witness the worst falling away of believers in the history of the church. **(2 Thes. 2:3-4, 1 Tim. 4:1)**

'Then a white robe was given to each of them; and it was said to them that they should rest a little while longer, until both the number of their fellow servants and their brethren, who would be killed as they were, was completed.' Revelation 6:11

Each martyr will receive a white robe! They are told to wait until the martyrdom of their brethren is completed. **(Rev. 6:9-11)** Notice these killed by the False Prophet have not yet received their incorruptible bodies. **(1 Cor. 15:52)** Which means, the resurrection of believers is near! **(Mat. 24:33, Rev. 7:9-17)** I ask you; how many faithful Christians will overcome during this time of testing? **(Rev. 3:5; 3:10)**

<u>How will it happen?</u>

'And I saw thrones, and they sat on them, and judgment was committed to them. Then I saw the souls of those who had been beheaded for their witness to Jesus and for the word of God, who had not worshiped the beast or his image, and had not received his mark on their foreheads or on their hands. And they lived and reigned with Christ for a thousand years.' Revelation 20:4

John saw the souls martyred for their witness of Jesus and the word of God! During the Great Tribulation, they will not worship the Beast! **(Rev. 20:4)** Instead they will receive a special reward for being faithful unto death. They will be resurrected on the first day of Christ's thousand-year reign over the nations! **(Rev. 20:6)** The spiritually saved during the Day of The Lord will also miss the Judgment Seat of Christ and the marriage to the Lamb. **(Rev. 11:18; 19:7)** When the Lamb and His wife arrive on a new earth, all saved from the nations will bring glory and honor into the New Jerusalem. **(Rev. 21:9-10, 23-27)**

Why will it matter?

"And he who overcomes, and keeps My works until the end, to him I will give power over the nations." Revelation 2:26

The fear of death will be overwhelming during the **Fourth** and **Fifth Seals**. **(Rev. 6:7-11)** The Christians unprepared for the persecution by the False Prophet will be targeted by demons through false teachers. **(Rev. 13:11-18, Mat. 24:4-5)** While the overcomers keeping His works till the harvest will be physically saved! **(Rev. 2:26, Mat. 13:39; 24:14)** Their love for God will be a strength in their greatest time of need! **(Rev. 3:10)** They will know who has the power to cast a sinner into hell! **(Luke 12:5)** Once again, how will Satan's wrath during the Great Tribulation be cut short before God's wrath during The Day of the Lord begins? **(Isa. 13:9-11)** Simply by understanding when the Son will gather His elect! **(Mark 13:23-27)**

"They shall neither hunger anymore nor thirst anymore; the sun shall not strike them, nor any heat; for the Lamb who is in the midst of the throne will shepherd them and lead them to living fountains of waters. And God will wipe away every tear from their eyes." Revelation 7:16-17

During the Great Tribulation, only the followers of the Beast will be able to buy or sell anything. **(Rev. 14:9-11)** Hunger and thirst will be a cross many Christians will have to bear during the **Fourth** and **Fifth Seals**. **(Rev. 6:7-11; 7:16-17)** His promise to shorten this persecution will give a great multitude the resolve to remain faithful even under the threat of death! **(Mat. 24:21-22, Rev. 7:9-17)**

'Let no one deceive you by any means; for that Day will not come unless the falling away comes first, and the man of sin is revealed, the son of perdition.' 2 Thes. 2:3

There are two ways false teachers are taking away from this teaching by Paul. They're prophesying this *'falling away coming first'* is not a departure from the faith by believers. **(2 Thes. 2:3)** Instead, they're teaching this departure is the resurrection of dead and alive believers before the Man of Sin is revealed! Beware saints, this is a twofold heresy! They're teaching a false gospel while taking away the timing from the Coming of our Lord Jesus Christ. **(2 Thes. 2:1-4)** Expecting our Blessed Hope before the mark of the Beast is forced on the world will become an eternal death sentence to so many! **(Rev. 14:9-11)**

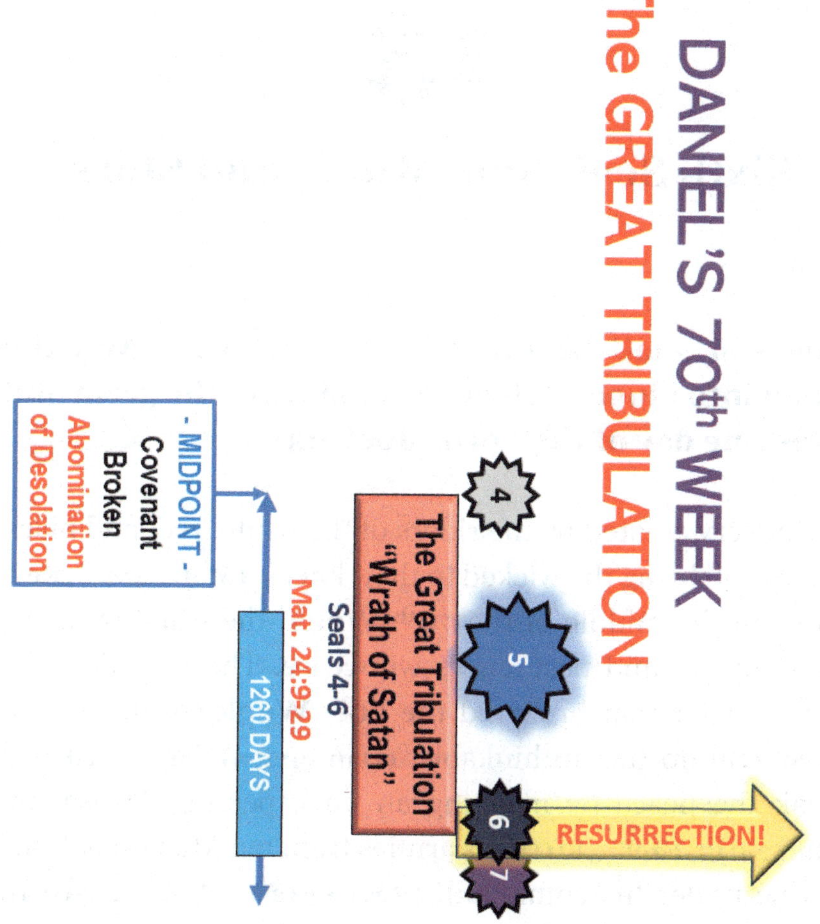
DANIEL'S 70th WEEK
The GREAT TRIBULATION
4
5
6
7
RESURRECTION!
The Great Tribulation
"Wrath of Satan"
Seals 4-6
Mat. 24:9-29
1260 DAYS
- MIDPOINT -
Covenant
Broken
Abomination
of Desolation

13

Sixth Seal: Sun, Moon, and Stars

'The sun shall be turned into darkness, And the moon into blood, Before the coming of the great and awesome day of the Lord.' Joel 2:31

The misery created by the riders of the white, red, and black horses will bring the wicked to their knees. **(Mat. 24:4-8, Rev. 6:1-6)** In the middle of the **70th Week**, the wars, famines, earthquakes, and pestilences will cease. The next day, the world leader that brokered the **70th Week** covenant with Israel will do the unthinkable. **(Dan. 9:27a)** The Beast will break the peace by invading an unsuspecting Jerusalem. **(Mat. 24:15, Ezek. 38:11)** His armies from ten Muslim nations will be under his command. **(Rev. 17:12-13, Luke 21:20)** In sheer panic, many will flee into the wilderness. **(Mat. 24:16-22, Rev. 12:6)** This invasion will initiate the Great Tribulation. **(Mat. 24:9-26)** On this same day, Death, the rider of the pale horse will come down to earth. **(Rev. 6:7-8)** This is when Satan will grant his power over the nations to the Beast. **(Rev. 13:3-5)** Anyone refusing to obey the Beast will face the persecution by the False Prophet. **(Rev. 13:11-18)** The agonizing division among Christian families will be devastating. **(Mat. 10:35)** To see so many saints overcome by the Beast will be unimaginable. **(Rev. 13:7)** After the opening of the **Fifth Seal**, John saw the faithful overcomers martyred during the Great Tribulation. **(Rev. 6:9-11)** Yet, he didn't fully understand the timing of these events until he saw the sign of The Day of The Lord. **(Isa. 13:9-11, Mat. 24:29)** The sun, moon, and stars losing their light. **(Rev. 6:12-17, Mark 13:24-27)**

<u>What is this event?</u>

'I looked when He opened the sixth seal, and behold, there was a great earthquake; and the sun became black as sackcloth of hair, and the moon became like blood. And the stars of heaven fell to the earth, as a fig tree drops its late figs when it is shaken by a mighty wind. Then the sky receded as a scroll when it is rolled up, and every mountain and island was moved out of its place.' Revelation 6:12-14

John suddenly felt a great earthquake. The sky was receding like a scroll. The stars were losing their light. The sun turned black. The moon a blood red. Mountains and islands were moving out of place. **(Rev. 6:12-14)** No man could do this. This will be the sign of The Day of The Lord. **(Isa. 13:9-10, Joel 2:30-31)** John watched for this sign for over sixty years. **(Luke 9:26-27, Mat. 24:29, Mark 13:24-25)** It never came until he saw it in a vision in 96 A.D.! **(Rev. 6:12-17)**

"And there will be signs in the sun, in the moon, and in the stars; and on the earth distress of nations, with perplexity, the sea and the waves roaring; men's hearts failing them from fear and the expectation of those things which are coming on the earth, for the powers of the heavens will be shaken. Then they will see the Son of Man coming in a cloud with power and great glory." Luke 21:25-27

The events from the **Fourth** and **Fifth Seals** will take place during the Great Tribulation! **(Rev. 6:7-11, Mat. 24:9-26)** After seeing men's hearts failing due to fear, John understood the timing of the Coming of The Son of Man. **(Luke 21:25-27)** When believers witness the powers of the heavens being shaken they will know the Lamb has just opened the **Sixth Seal**! **(Rev. 6:12-17)** The sign of the Day of The Lord. **(Isa. 13:9-11, Mark 13:23-27)**

Who is involved?

'...Fall on us and hide us from the face of Him who sits on the throne and from the wrath of the Lamb. For the great day of His wrath has come, and who is able to stand?' Revelation 6:16-17

Trapped in darkness, the wicked will think the wrath of the Lamb has come. In this verse, 'has come' is about a future event, not a completed action. **(Rev. 6:17)** Remember when Judas betrayed Jesus in the Garden of Gethsemane. **(Mark 14:41-43)** As the traitor arrived with soldiers, Jesus told His disciples His hour 'has come'. Had Jesus faced Pilate? No, His trial was in the immediate future. After the **Sixth Seal**, Jesus will send forth angels to gather believers from heaven and earth. **(Mark 13:24-27)** On this same day **(Luke 17:30)**, thirty minutes after the opening of the **Seventh Seal**, the Day of The Lord will begin with fire! **(Rev. 8:1-5)**

When will it happen?

"But take heed to yourselves, lest your hearts be weighed down with carousing, drunkenness, and cares of this life, and that Day come on you unexpectedly. For it will come as a snare on all those who dwell on the face of the whole earth." Luke 21:34-35

When will the Great Tribulation be cut short? **(Mat. 24:21-22)** The day the constellations lose their light **(Rev. 6:12-17; 7:9-17)** God will make a speedy riddance of sinners dwelling in the land. **(Luke 21:34-36)** Old Testament prophets foretold this sign will usher in God's wrath upon the wicked. **(Isa. 13:9-11, Zep. 1:18)** So did our Lord. **(Mark 13:24-27)** The day the wicked experience the sign of the Day of The Lord, every eye will see the sign of The Son of Man. **(Rev. 1:7, Mat. 24:29-31)**

'..."These are the ones who come out of the great tribulation, and washed their robes and made them white in the blood of the Lamb." Revelation 7:14

In his vision, John then saw a great multitude from every nation standing before the throne of God. **(Rev. 7:9-17)** These blood-washed saints have just come out of the Great Tribulation. **(Rev. 6:7-11)** They have incorruptible bodies. **(1 Cor. 15:50-52)** Their praising the Father and the Lamb for their salvation. **(Rev. 7:9-14)**

'The lofty looks of man shall be humbled, The haughtiness of men shall be bowed down, And the Lord alone shall be exalted in that day.' Isaiah 2:11

Immediately after the suffering (tribulation) from the first five seals **(Mat. 24:4-26, Rev. 6:1-11)**, the sun, moon, and stars will lose their light. **(Rev. 6:12-17, Mat. 24:29)** Satan knows what this means. The resurrection of overcomers has cut short His wrath during the Great Tribulation. **(Rev. 7:9-17; 12:12; 13:1-18)** Only Jesus will be exalted during, the Day of The Lord. (**Isa. 2:11**) Every Christian needs to understand this sequence of events. (**Rev. 6:1-17; 7:9-17; 8:1-5)**

"See, I have told you beforehand." Matthew 24:25

There are no scriptures supporting the resurrection of dead and alive believers to heaven before (Pre), in the middle (Mid) or at the end (Post) of the **70th Week** of Daniel. **(Dan. 9:24-27)** So how is Satan using these man-made deceptions to deceive believers? By taking away the timing of the Coming of The Son of Man. **(Luke 21:8)** The only time the future bride of Christ is delivered out of the Great Tribulation will be during the second half of the **70th Week.** **(Rev. 6:12-17; 7:9-17)** Jesus has told us the day He will come back. **(Mat. 24:25)** After the darkness from the **Sixth Seal** covers the earth during the Feast of Trumpets **(Mat. 24:29-36, Mark 13:24-27),** every eye will see the Son coming in the glory of His Father. **(Rev. 1:7, Mat. 16:27)**

"He who rejects Me, and does not receive My words, has that which judges him— the word that I have spoken will judge him in the last day." John 12:48

Since the 1970's, popular end time teachers have made millions of dollars vainly prophesying the timing of the resurrection. **(John 12:48)** They have used blood moons, major storms, even eclipses to somehow represent the future **Sixth Seal**. **(Mat. 24:29, Rev. 6:12-17)** So many were convinced they would be caught up! Until the next day when nothing happened! Trying to reach them with the truth is no easy task. God will forgive them if they would repent. It will be a different outcome during the darkness of the Great Tribulation! **(Luke 21:25-27)** When the Son of Man comes back, all denying their faith will have no excuse. **(Luke 21:8)**

"But in those days, after that tribulation, the sun will be darkened, and the moon will not give its light; the stars of heaven will fall, and the powers in the heavens will be shaken. Then they will see the Son of Man coming in the clouds with great power and glory. And then He will send His angels, and gather together His elect from the four winds, from the farthest part of earth to the farthest part of heaven." Mark 13:24-27

Since 1990, I've taught how the Son of Man will initiate His Second Coming. **(Mark 13:24-27)** Watching deceiving spirits plant false interpretations taking away the consequences of the resurrection has been a heartbreak. This is why many have given up trying to understand the timing of our redemption. **(Luke 21:34-36)** We often hear, *"It doesn't matter when Jesus comes back, I'm saved."* Surely, if one is saved, they're ready to die and go to heaven! Yet, every saint overcome by the Beast will miss the harvest at the Coming of The Son of Man. **(Rev. 13:7)**

How will it happen?

'Then he opened his mouth in blasphemy against God, to blaspheme His name, His tabernacle, and those who dwell in heaven.' Revelation 13:6

The day his armies surround Jerusalem **(Luke 21:20)**, the Beast will blaspheme the Name of God, His tabernacle, and those dwelling in heaven. **(Mat. 24:15, Rev. 13:5-6)** When

Christians hear this sacrilege, they will know the Great Tribulation is underway. **(2 Thes. 2:3-4)** So how will the Son of Man cut short this horrific persecution? **(Mat. 24:21-22)** The day the heavens lose their light **(Mark 13:24-27)**; a great multitude of overcomers will come out of the Great Tribulation and stand before the throne of God in heaven! **(Rev. 7:9-17)** That same day God will begin destroying sinners left behind! **(Isa. 13:9-11, Luke 17:30, Rev. 8:1-2)**

"Immediately after the tribulation of those days the sun will be darkened, and the moon will not give its light; the stars will fall from heaven, and the powers of the heavens will be shaken." Matthew 24:29

John witnessed the Lamb opening the seven seals of the heavenly scroll. **(Rev. 6:1-17; 8:1)** These events will take place inside the **70th Week**. **(Mat. 24:3-33)** The first three seals will be opened in the first half of this seven year covenant with Israel. **(Rev. 6:1-6)** The last four seals in the second half! **(Rev. 6:7-17; 8:1)**

<u>The Beginning of Sorrows</u>

First Seal, the deception of many believers! **(Mat. 24:4-5)**
Second Seal, the horrific spreading of wars! **(Mat. 24:6)**
Third Seal, famines, earthquakes, and pestilences! **(Mat. 24:7-8)**

<u>The Great Tribulation</u>

Fourth Seal, Satan's wrath against believers! **(Mat. 24:9-22)**
Fifth Seal, martyrs dying for Jesus! **(Mat. 24:9-13)**

Sixth Seal, constellations losing their light! **(Mat. 24:29)**

<u>The Day of The Lord</u>

Seventh Seal, the wrath of The Lamb! **(Mat. 24:37-39)**

John recognized the sign of the Day of The Lord. **(Isa. 13:9-11, Mat. 24:29, Rev. 6:12-17)** The day angels gather believers out of this darkness, the earth will begin to burn with fire. **(Mark 13:24-27, Rev. 8:1-7)** A revelation rarely taught today!

<u>Why will it matter?</u>

'They will give an account to Him who is ready to judge the living and the dead.' 1 Peter 4:5

Popular teachers often use the scare tactic: *"You better be ready; our Lord could split the eastern sky right now."* They even smile while rebuking believers refusing to accept this lie! Others confidently threaten, *"You will have to give an account to God for such appalling neglect."* **(1 Pet. 4:5)** Most have no idea they're deceiving the body of Christ. **(Rev. 22:19)** Jesus plainly teaches the only time the physical redemption of believers can come is after the sun, moon, and stars lose their light. **(Mark 13:23-27, Luke 21:25-28)**

'When the Lord Jesus is revealed from heaven with His mighty angels, in flaming fire taking vengeance on those who do not know God, and on those who do not obey the gospel of our Lord Jesus Christ. These shall be punished with everlasting destruction from the presence of the Lord and from the glory of His power.' 2 Thessalonians 1:7-9

When Jesus is revealed in flaming fire with His mighty angels, who will suffer His vengeance? **(2 Thes. 1:7-9)** There will be two groups. **(Mat. 13:39-42)**
The wicked who never knew God.
The apostates no longer obeying the gospel!
They will be punished with everlasting destruction from the presence of the Lord.

The Sign of The Day of The Lord

What will happen the day the Lamb opens the **Sixth Seal**?

1. The wicked will be worshiping the Beast.
2. The sun, moon, and stars will lose their light.
3. The Son will come back in the glory of His Father.
4. The resurrection of believers from heaven and earth.
5. The Great Tribulation will end.
6. The Seventh Seal will be opened.
7. The world will suffer the Day of The Lord.

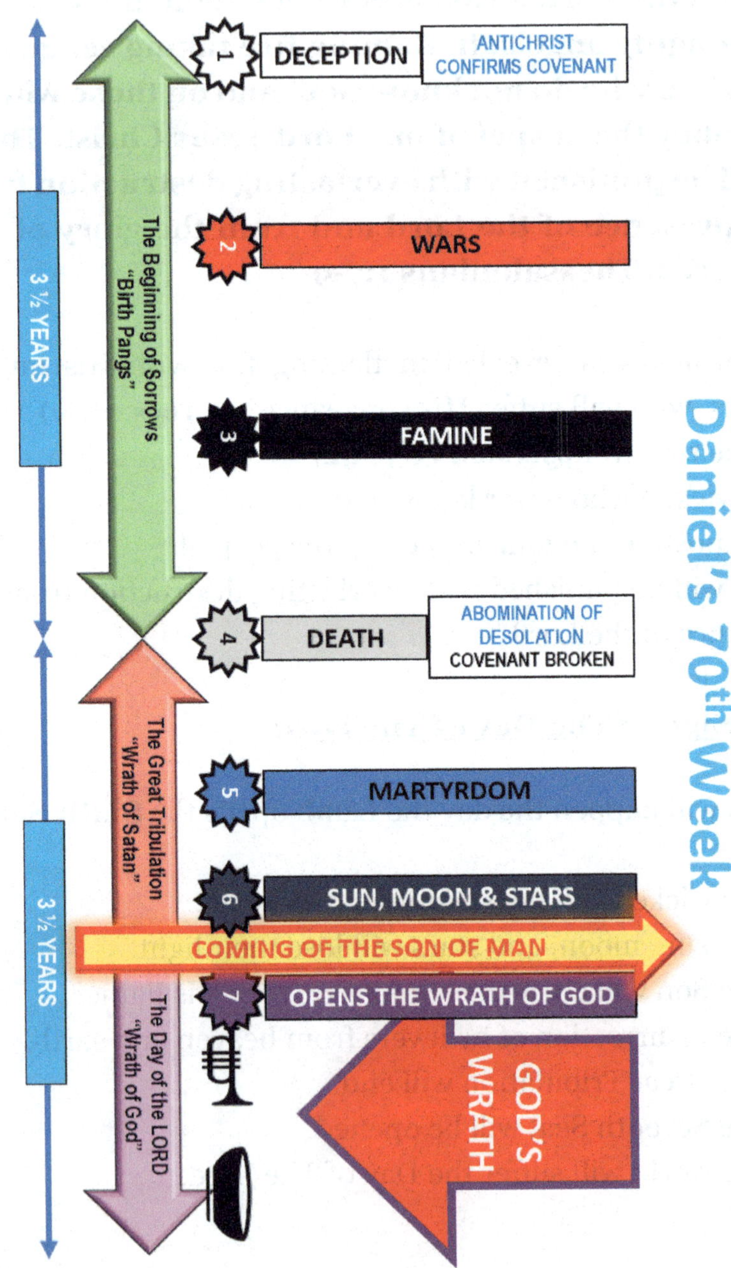

Daniel's 70th Week
3 ½ YEARS
3 ½ YEARS
The Beginning of Sorrows
"Birth Pangs"
The Great Tribulation
"Wrath of Satan"
The Day of the LORD
"Wrath of God"
1
DECEPTION
ANTICHRIST
CONFIRMS COVENANT
2
WARS
3
FAMINE
4
DEATH
ABOMINATION OF
DESOLATION
COVENANT BROKEN
5
MARTYRDOM
6
SUN, MOON & STARS
COMING OF THE SON OF MAN
7
OPENS THE WRATH OF GOD
GOD'S
WRATH

14

A Great Multitude From Every Nation

'For this we say to you by the word of the Lord, that we who are alive and remain until the coming of the Lord will by no means precede those who are asleep.' 1 Thessalonians 4:15

Jesus told John when He will gather His elect. **(Luke 21:25-28)** Shrouded in darkness **(Mat. 24:29, Rev. 6:12-17)**, the wicked will mourn after witnessing the sign of the Son of Man. **(Mat. 24:30)** Every eye will see the Son coming in the clouds. **(Rev. 1:7, Mat. 16:27)** At the trump of God, Jesus will send forth His angels to gather believers from heaven and earth. **(Mark 13:24-27, 1 Thes. 4:15-17)** This was a new revelation! An event John was expecting to happen at any moment. **(Rev. 7:9-17)**

What is this event?

'After these things I looked, and behold, a great multitude which no one could number, of all nations, tribes, peoples, and tongues, standing before the throne and before the Lamb, clothed with white robes, with palm branches in their hands... Salvation belongs to our God who sits on the throne, and to the Lamb!" Revelation 7:9-10

During the Great Tribulation, a terrified world will be hiding in darkness. **(Mat. 24:21-22, 29, Rev. 6:12-17)** At any moment, every eye will see the Son coming in the glory of His Father. **(Rev. 1:7, Mat. 16:27, Mark 13:24-27)** Believers from heaven are with Jesus. **(1 Thes. 4:13-16)** In the twinkling of an eye, dead and alive saints will receive incorruptible bodies. **(1 Cor. 15:50-52)** After this, John sees a great multitude standing before the Father and the Lamb in heaven. **(Rev. 7:9-10)**

'These are the ones who come out of the great tribulation, and washed their robes and made them white in the blood of the Lamb.' Revelation 7:14

John understood the timing of the resurrection of alive believers. **(Mark 13:24-27)** After the Son of Man is seen in glory, a great multitude of overcomers from every nation will come out of the Great Tribulation. **(Mat. 16:27, Rev. 7:9-17)** They will stand before the Father and the Lamb in heaven. Paul also taught when alive believers will be caught up. **(1 Thes. 4:17)** Before the gathering of believers to Jesus, the

Man of Sin will be revealed during the Great Tribulation. **(2 Thes. 2:1-4)** Tragically, many coming in His name are denying this revelation. Jesus is exhorting us not to follow after them. **(Luke 21:8)** The only time angels can gather believers out of the Great Tribulation is after the constellations lose their light! **(Rev. 6:12-17; 7:9-17)** The sign of The Day of The Lord **(Mat. 24:29)** followed by the sign of the Son of Man **(Mat. 24:30)** on the same day. **(Luke 17:26-30)**

Who is involved?

"For whoever is ashamed of Me and My words in this adulterous and sinful generation, of him the Son of Man also will be ashamed when He comes in the glory of His Father with the holy angels."
Mark 8:38

Who will be ashamed of the Son of Man when He comes in the glory of His Father? **(Mark 8:38)** Sadly, it will be the former believers following the Beast. **(Mat. 25:31-46)** Finally realizing what they have done, they will cry out in despair. Their pleas for mercy will not be answered. This adulterous generation will not escape the wrath of the Lamb of God! **(Isa. 13:9-11, Rev. 6:16-17; 8:1-5)**

"For then there will be great tribulation, such as has not been since the beginning of the world until this time, no, nor ever shall be. And unless those days were shortened, no flesh would be saved; but for the elect's sake those days will be shortened."
Mathew 24:21-22

Jesus has already told us how the Coming of The Son of Man will shorten the Great Tribulation. **(Mat. 24:21-22, 30-31, 40-41)** At His Coming, all believers will be caught up before the wrath of the Lamb is poured out on the wicked left behind. **(Rev. 6:16-17; 7:9-17; 8:1-2)** Which means the church won't face God's wrath during The Day of The Lord. **(Rev. 8:1-5; 15:1; 16:1-21)** This explains the spiritual warfare blinding so many from understanding this revelation. **(1 Thes. 5:4-9)**

When will it happen?

'They shall neither hunger anymore nor thirst anymore; the sun shall not strike them nor any heat; for the Lamb who is in the midst of the throne will shepherd them and lead them to living fountains of waters. And God will wipe away every tear from their eyes.' Revelation 7:16-17

Satan's great wrath during the Great Tribulation will cease after the opening of the **Sixth Seal**. **(Mat. 24:29-31, Rev. 12:12)** From this darkness, a great multitude will be caught up before the throne of God. These overcomers will never hunger or thirst again. God will wipe away their tears while leading them to living fountains of water. **(Rev. 7:16-17)**

<u>How will it happen?</u>

'Then we who are alive and remain shall be caught up together with them in the clouds to meet the Lord in the air. And thus we shall always be with the Lord.' 1 Thessalonians 4:17

How will believers be delivered out of the Great Tribulation? **(Mat. 24:21-22)** 'Remain' in this passage means 'survive.' **(1 Thes. 4:17)** The overcomers surviving the horrifying persecution by the Beast will be caught up in the clouds with the dead in Christ! **(Rev. 7:9-17)** This is how our Blessed Hope will initiate the Day of The Lord **(Mark 13:24-27)**, the wrath of the Lamb. **(Titus 2:13)**

"And behold, I am coming quickly, and My reward is with Me, to give to every one according to his work." Revelation 22:12

So how are pastors denying the resurrection of believers out of the Great Tribulation? **(Rev. 7:9-17)** Instead, they're teaching this great multitude are somehow martyrs. Yet, John witnessed the martyrs from the Great Tribulation after the opening of the **Fifth Seal**. **(Rev. 6:9-11)** These alive overcomers will arrive in heaven together. While martyrs will come out one at a time! Beware saints, taking away the timing of the resurrection has eternal consequences. **(Rev. 22:19)**

<u>Why will it matter?</u>

'But you, brethren, are not in darkness, so that this Day should overtake you as a thief.'
1 Thessalonians 5:4

The only way to cut short the Great Tribulation is by removing the object of the persecution. **(Rev. 7:9-14)** The day believers are caught up to heaven during the Feast of Trumpets, God's wrath will erupt on earth! **(Mat. 24:36-39, Isa. 13:9-11)**

When the armies of the Beast surround Jerusalem, the faithful overcomers won't be in darkness. **(Luke 21:20, 1 Thes. 5:4)**

When the Man of Sin exalts himself in the temple of God, the overcomers won't be in darkness. **(2 Thes. 2:1-4)**

When the False Prophet is killing believers, the overcomers won't be in darkness.
(Rev. 13:11-18, Mat. 24:13)

When the world sees the sign of The Son of Man, the overcomers will be looking up for their redemption. **(Mat. 16:27, Luke 21:27-28)**

'Which is manifest evidence of the righteous judgment of God, that you may be counted worthy of the kingdom of God, for which you also suffer.'
2 Thessalonians 2:5

Who will be counted worthy for the kingdom of God? **(2 Thes. 2:5)** Most have been taught all having the testimony of Jesus will never suffer the Great Tribulation! **(Rev. 12:12, 17)** This is why they won't be expecting persecution from their own family during Satan's great wrath. **(Mat. 10:34-36; 24:9-13)** They just can't see the need for the Son to righteously judge the goats from His sheep. **(Mat. 25:31-42)**

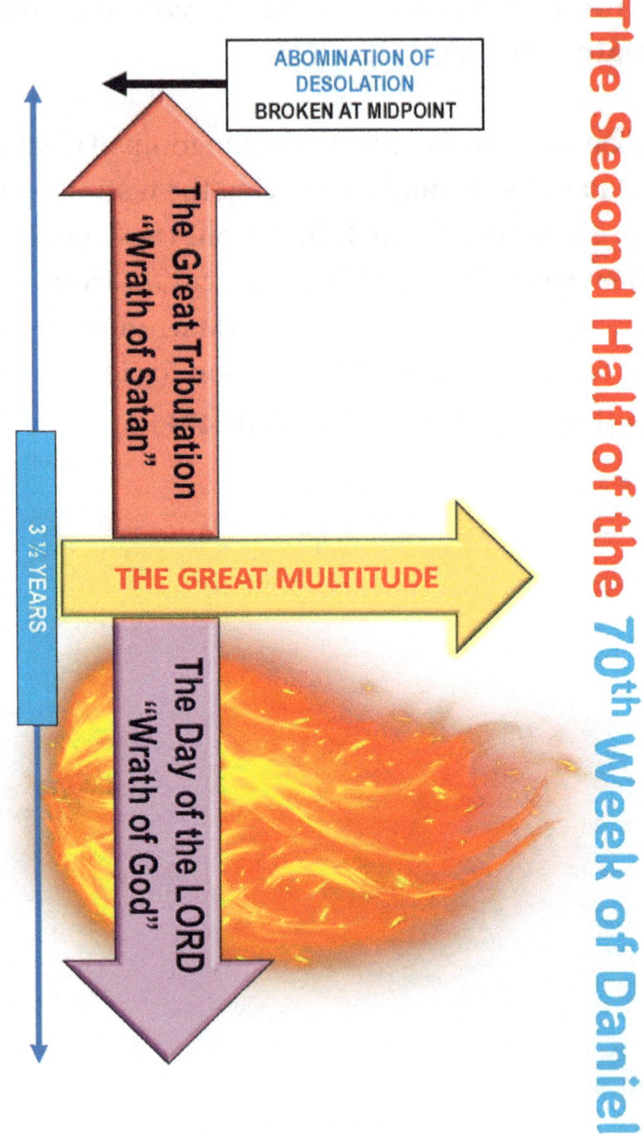

The Second Half of the 70th Week of Daniel
ABOMINATION OF DESOLATION
BROKEN AT MIDPOINT
The Great Tribulation
"Wrath of Satan"
THE GREAT MULTITUDE
The Day of the LORD
"Wrath of God"
3 ½ YEARS

15

Coming of The Son of Man

"Therefore you also be ready, for the Son of Man is coming at an hour you do not expect."
Matthew 24:44

Since 1990, I've asked thousands of Christians to describe the events Jesus will fulfill during His Second Coming? Why is it, I rarely received a scriptural reply? This demonic warfare is so obvious. This is why there will be such a lack of faith when the Son of Man gathers His elect from the wrath to come. **(Luke 18:8)** The night before He died for the sins of the world, He gave us a promise. **(John 14:1-4)** The Son was leaving to prepare a place for His bride. It's called the holy Jerusalem. At His Coming, the Son will deliver faithful believers from the wrath to come. **(Rev. 7:9-17)** Later, they will be rewarded at the Judgment Seat of Christ. **(Rev. 11:18)** Before being married to the Lamb of God. **(Rev. 19:7)** His Second Coming will end after the Lamb and His wife descend to a new earth inside a new heaven to rule for 1,000 years. **(Rev. 20:6; 21:9-10)**

What is this event?

"Then they will see the Son of Man coming in the clouds with great power and glory. And then He will send His angels, and gather together His elect from the four winds, from the farthest part of earth to the farthest part of heaven." Mark 13:26-27

John listened as Jesus described the future resurrection of dead and alive believers. **(Matthew 24-25, Mark 13, Luke 21)** Our Lord began by teaching the events that will take place before the Coming of The Son of Man. **(Mat. 24:3-33)** His description of the Beginning of Sorrows followed by the days of the Great Tribulation were illustrative and shocking. **(Mat. 24:4-8, 9-22)** The world will be cloaked in darkness when they see the Son coming in the glory of His Father. **(Mat. 24:29-30)** At any moment, angels will gather believers from heaven and earth. **(1 Cor. 15:50-52, Mark 13:24-27)** This same day, the wrath of the Lamb will begin punishing the world for its evil. **(Mat. 24:37-39, Rev. 6:16-17; 8:1-2)**

Who is involved?

"...These are the ones who come out of the great tribulation, and washed their robes and made them white in the blood of the Lamb." Revelation 7:14b

Three nights before His death, Jesus was concerned for the safety of believers living during the future Great Tribulation. How many times have you heard, *"No one knows when the Son of Man will come back for us?"* Yet, Jesus has already told us when He will gather His elect. **(Mat. 24:25)** This is the only time the resurrection can happen at any moment! The day the sun, moon, and stars lose their light during the Feast of Trumpets, every eye will see the Son of Man coming back in the clouds of heaven! **(Mat. 24:29-36)**

'Jesus said to him, "It is as you said. Nevertheless, I say to you, hereafter you will see the Son of Man sitting at the right hand of the Power, and coming on the clouds of heaven." Matthew 26:64

We often hear, *"The Coming of the Son of Man is only for Israel."* (False)

During His ministry, Jesus taught the Coming of the Son of Man **(Mat. 24:30-31)**, the Lord's Supper **(Mat. 26:26-28)**, and the Great Commission **(Mat. 28:17-20)**. These ordinances are instruction for all abiding in Christ. **(Eph. 3:5-7)**

When will it happen?

"Immediately after the tribulation of those days the sun will be darkened, and the moon will not give its light; the stars will fall from heaven, and the powers of the heavens will be shaken. Then the sign of the Son of Man will appear in heaven, and then all the tribes of the earth will mourn, and they will see the Son of Man coming on the clouds of heaven with power and great glory." Matthew 24:29-30

The Coming of the Son of Man will be like the days of Noah. **(Luke 17:26-30)** The same day the righteous are delivered, the unrighteous will suffer the wrath of God. **(Mat. 24:37-39)** So, when can we expect to see Jesus? Our Lord is exhorting us to watch for two signs. The sign of the Day of The Lord followed by the sign of The Son of Man. **(Mat. 24:29-30)** The same day a great multitude of overcomers come out of the Great Tribulation **(Rev. 7:9-17)**; a terrified world cloaked in darkness will suffer the wrath of the Lamb. **(Rev. 6:16-17; 8:1-2)**

"Then if anyone says to you, 'Look, here is the Christ!' or 'There!' do not believe it. For false christs and false prophets will rise and show great signs and wonders to deceive, if possible, even the elect. See I have told you beforehand. Therefore if they say to you, 'Look, He is in the desert.' do not go out; or 'Look, He is in the inner rooms.' do not believe it." Matthew 24:23-26

During the Great Tribulation, false christs and false prophets will deceive many by performing great signs and wonders. **(Mat. 24:21-26)** Others will gain a following by prophesying Jesus is on the earth. Don't believe them! **(Deut. 18:22)** Jesus won't touch the earth at His Coming. **(Luke 21:25-28)** Instead, every eye will see the Son coming with the clouds, in the glory of His Father. **(Rev. 1:7, Mat. 16:27)**

'In a moment, in the twinkling of an eye, at the last trumpet. For the trumpet will sound, and the dead will be raised incorruptible, and we shall be changed.' 1 Corinthians 15:51

There is another popular premise taking away the timing of the resurrection. Many are convinced the sounding of the **Seventh Trumpet** is the last trumpet. **(Rev. 11:15)** Is this true? **(1 Cor. 15:50-52)** The actual last trumpet in scripture will sound just before the 1,000 year reign of Christ begins. **(Rev. 20:6; 21:9-10)** Saved Jews are returning to Zion to worship the Lord in the rebuilt House of God. **(Isa. 27:12-13)** Clearly, this isn't the resurrection of believers out of the Great Tribulation. Which has already taken place after the **Sixth Seal**. **(Rev. 7:9-17)** Exactly where Jesus places the last trump blown by God! **(Mat. 24:29-31)** Whereas an angel will sound the **Seventh Trumpet** during the Day of The Lord. **(Rev. 11:15)**

How will it happen?

"Then they will deliver you up to tribulation and kill you, and you will be hated by all nations for My name's sake. And then many will be offended, will betray one another, and will hate one another." Matthew 24:9-10

Three nights before His death, Jesus taught the most comprehensive teaching on, The Coming of The Son of Man. **(Mat. 24-25, Mark 13, Luke 21)** His major concern is the salvation of believers living during the Great Tribulation. **(Mat. 24:9-10)** This is why Jesus told us the very day He will shorten it. The persecution by the two beasts will cease the day the sun, moon, and stars lose their light! Isaiah calls this sign, the Day of The Lord. **(Isa. 13:9-11, Mat. 24:29-31)**

'For the Lord Himself will descend from heaven with a shout, with the voice of an archangel, and with the trumpet of God. And the dead in Christ will rise first. Then we who are alive and remain shall be caught up together with them in the clouds to meet the Lord in the air…' 1 Thessalonians 4:16-17

Paul describes how believers will be caught up at the Coming of our Lord. **(1 Thes. 4:13-17)** Jesus will descend from heaven with a shout. The dead in Christ will be with Him. At the last trumpet, their dead bodies in the graves will rise first! **(1 Thes. 4:13-16)** In the twinkling of an eye, they will receive incorruptible bodies. **(1 Cor. 15:50-52)** Then a great multitude of overcomers will be caught up out of the Great Tribulation. **(Rev. 7:9-17)** They will all be gathered together to meet their Lord in the air. **(1 Thes. 4:17, Mark 13:26-27)**

Why will it matter?

'Then the seventh angel poured out his bowl into the air, and a loud voice came out of the temple of heaven, from the throne, saying, "It is done!" Revelation 16:17

The Coming of the Son of Man will take place **after** the opening of the **Sixth Seal. (Mat. 24:29, Rev. 6:12-17; 7:9-17)** The appearing of the Word of God will take place **after** the pouring out of the **Seventh Bowl**! **(Rev. 15:1; 16:17; 19:11-21)** Jesus will fulfill these two events during His Second Coming. I emphasize again, anyone teaching the Second Coming is a single event is deceiving the body of Christ!

'It was granted to him to make war with the saints and to overcome them. And authority was given him over every tribe, tongue, and nation.'
Revelation 13:7

On a typical Sunday morning you will hear this popular deception:

"No Christian will ever be overcome by the Beast!" (False) So how will the Beast overcome many saints before the harvest? **(Rev. 13:7, Mat. 13:39-42)** Tragically, to avoid persecution, there may be more Christians choosing to obey the Beast than those getting the victory. **(Rev. 3:5, Mat. 25:31-46)**

'Now as He sat on the Mount of Olives opposite the temple, Peter, James, John, and Andrew asked Him privately, "Tell us, when will these things be? And what will be the sign when all these things will be fulfilled?" Mark 13:3

Days before His death, Jesus taught the events that will take place before the Coming of The Son of Man. **(Mat. 24:3-33)** He entrusted His disciples to teach these glorious truths to those having ears to hear! **(Mark 13:3)** Imagine the conversations they may have had while sharing what they learned. Revelations most pastors are not teaching today!

"Therefore when you see the 'abomination of desolation,' spoken of by Daniel the prophet, standing in the holy place" (whoever reads, let him understand)." Matthew 24:15

"I was there that night. Jesus quoted Daniel. Our Lord is warning believers to be watching for the Abomination of Desolation. After his armies surround Jerusalem, this deceiver will stand in the holy place. A terrible time when many will flee to the mountains. Yes, this persecution will take place before the Coming of the Son of Man." PETER

"Then the sign of the Son of Man will appear in heaven, and then all the tribes of the earth will mourn, and they will see the Son of Man coming on the clouds of heaven with power and great glory." Matthew 24:30

"While on the Mount of Olives, Jesus taught us the sign of the Son of Man. It will look like lightning flashing from the east to the west. The wicked will mourn when they see the Son coming with power and great glory!" JAMES

"And then He will send His angels, and gather together His elect from the four winds, from the farthest part of earth to the farthest part of heaven." Mark 13:27

"I've always believed only the dead will be raised on the last day. That is until I heard Jesus' share what will happen at His Coming. The Son of Man will begin by sending forth His angels. These reapers will gather together alive believers from earth with the dead in Christ from heaven. Yes, everyone will be rewarded according to their works at the Judgment Seat of Christ!" JOHN

"All these are the beginning of sorrows...For then there will be great tribulation, such as has not been since the beginning of the world until this time..." Matthew 24:8, 21

"While on the Mount of Olives, Jesus told us what will take place before He comes back. Our Lord calls these events the Beginning of Sorrows followed by the days of the Great Tribulation. It's true, everyone should be watching for these events before the Coming of the Son of Man!" ANDREW

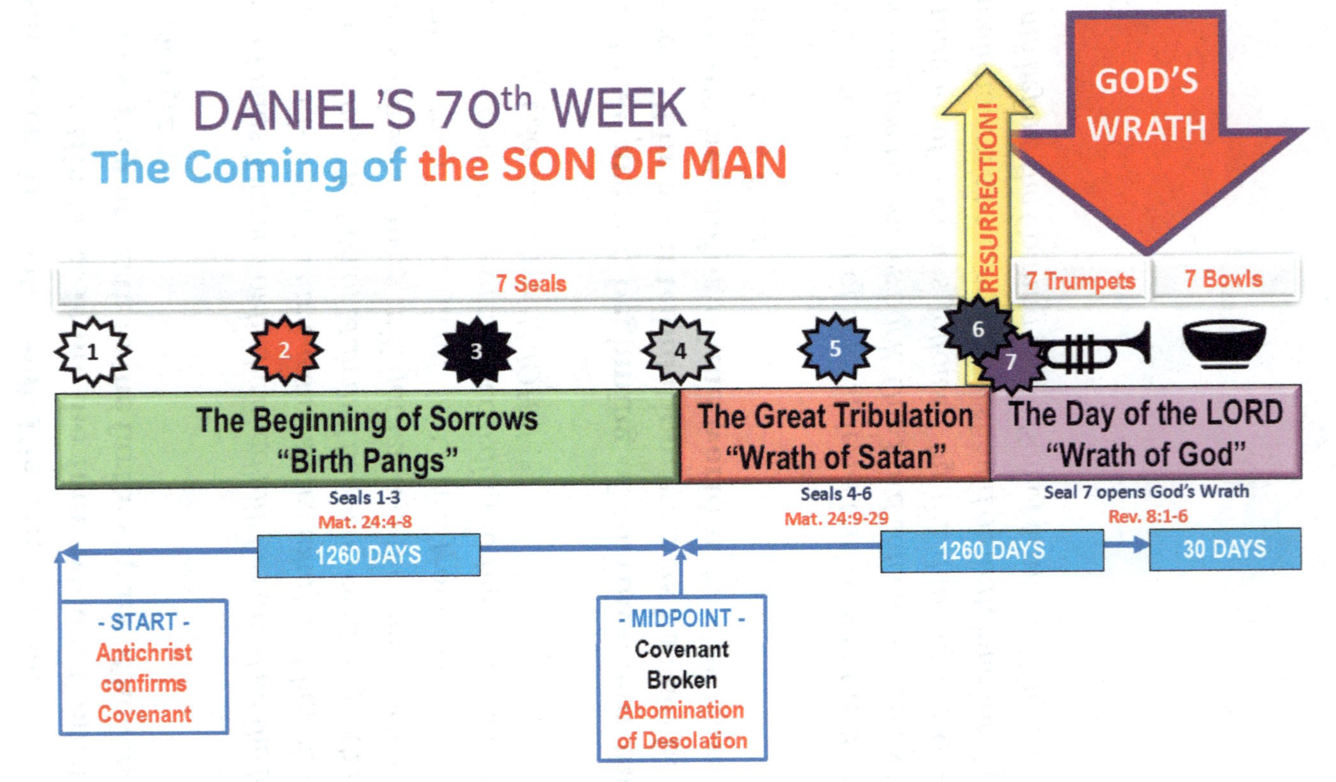

DANIEL'S 70th WEEK
The Coming of the SON OF MAN
GOD'S WRATH
RESURRECTION!
7 Seals
7 Trumpets
7 Bowls
1
2
3
4
5
6
7
The Beginning of Sorrows
"Birth Pangs"
The Great Tribulation
"Wrath of Satan"
The Day of the LORD
"Wrath of God"
Seals 1-3
Mat. 24:4-8
Seals 4-6
Mat. 24:9-29
Seal 7 opens God's Wrath
Rev. 8:1-6
1260 DAYS
1260 DAYS
30 DAYS
- START -
Antichrist
confirms
Covenant
- MIDPOINT -
Covenant
Broken
Abomination
of Desolation

16

Goats From The Sheep

'... 'I will open My mouth in parables; I will utter things kept secret from the foundation of the world." Matthew 13:35

Why did our Lord teach parables? Parables revealing things kept secret from the foundation of the world. **(Mat. 13:35)** A parable is a simple story highlighting a biblical truth. The intent is to teach the mysteries of the kingdom to those having ears to hear. **(Mat. 13:10-12)** During His Olivet Discourse, Jesus taught four parables. Each describes the consequences of, The Coming of The Son of Man!

"Now learn this parable from the fig tree: When its branch has already become tender and puts forth leaves, you know that summer is near. So you also, when you see all these things, know that it is near—at the doors." Matthew 24:32-33

(1) The Fig Tree

Our Lord used a fig tree to describe the nearness of His Second Coming. **(Mat. 24:30-33)** When the branches on a fig tree become tender and put forth leaves, the summer is near. In the same way, the moment the heavens lose their light, every eye will see the sign of the Son of Man. **(Mat. 24:29-30, Rev. 1:7)** Jesus is coming back in the glory of His Father! **(Mat. 16:27)** Overcomers experiencing the Great Tribulation will be looking up for their redemption! **(Rev. 7:9-17, Luke 21:28)**

"Who then is a faithful and wise servant, whom his master made ruler over his household, to give them due season? Blessed is that servant whom his master, when he comes, will find so doing. Assuredly, I say to you that he will make him ruler over all his goods. But if that evil servant says in his heart, 'My master is delaying his coming,' and begins to beat his fellow servants, and to eat and drink with the drunkards, the master of that servant will come on a day when he is not looking for him and at an hour that he is not aware of, and will cut him in two and appoint him his portion with the hypocrites. There shall be weeping and gnashing of teeth." Matthew 24:45-51

(2) The Unfaithful Servant

The next parable is about a faithful servant becoming evil. While His Master is away, he begins to drink with drunkards and beat his fellow servants! His Master will come back on a day he is not expecting! An hour he is not aware of. After the Coming of The Son of Man, he will be cast into everlasting fire, where there is weeping and gnashing of teeth! **(Mat. 24:45-51; 25:41-46)**

"Then the kingdom of heaven shall be likened to ten virgins who took their lamps and went out to meet the bridegroom. Now five of them were wise, and five were foolish...Watch therefore, for you know neither the day nor the hour in which the Son of Man is coming." Matthew 25:1-2, 13

(3) The Ten Virgins

The third parable is a story about ten virgins. They're supposed to be watching for their future bridegroom. Yet, five are wise and five are foolish. The wise believers have oil in their lamps, while the foolish no longer have any oil. When the bridegroom returns, the faithful believers will enter the kingdom of heaven. Sadly, the virgins with no oil will miss the marriage to the Lamb of God! **(Mat. 25:1-13)**

'For to everyone who has, more will be given, and he will have abundance; but from him who does not have, even what he has will be taken away. And cast the unprofitable servant into the outer darkness. There will be weeping and gnashing of teeth.' Matthew 25:29-30

(4) The Talents

The fourth parable is about three servants who were given talents. **(Mat. 25:14-30)** When Jesus comes back, the two servants found faithful will enter into the joy of their Lord. The unprofitable servant will be cast into outer darkness! Where there is weeping and gnashing of teeth. Again, this is a frightening picture of apostates being cursed into everlasting fire! **(Mat. 25:41)**

"Therefore, I speak to them in parables, because seeing they do not see, and hearing they do not hear, nor do they understand." Matthew 13:13

Why are most Christians not understanding these parables? **(Mat. 24:32-33, 45-51; 25:1-13, 14-30)** They have read them many times. They often hear how important they are. Yet, something is preventing them from grasping the truth! Are they willfully ignorant? Jesus gives us the answer by quoting the prophet Isaiah!

'And in them the prophecy of Isaiah is fulfilled, which says: 'Hearing you will hear and shall not understand, And seeing you will see and not perceive; For the hearts of this people have grown dull. Their ears are hard of hearing, And their eyes they have closed, Lest they should see with their eyes and hear with their ears, Lest they should understand with their hearts and turn, So that I should heal them.' Matthew 13:14-15

'For the time will come when they will not endure sound doctrine, but according to their own desires, because they have itching ears, they will heap up for themselves teachers.' 2 Timothy 4:3

So what is the main point of these parables? Jesus is highlighting the difference between those abiding in Him and those denying Him! **(Mat. 25:31-32)** Enduring sound doctrine is no longer a priority for many professing Christ! **(1 Tim. 4:1)** The exhortation to continually abide in the doctrine of Christ is rarely heard! **(2 John 1:9-10)** The result, many having itching ears are being deceived by false teachers bringing destructive heresies denying their Lord. **(2 Pet. 2:1)** So why aren't believers learning these parables? For many, fulfilling their own desires is more important than obeying the warnings by Jesus! **(2 Tim. 4:3)**

What is this event?

"When the Son of Man comes in His glory, and all the holy angels with Him, then He will sit on the throne of His glory...And He will set the sheep on His right hand, but the goats on the left...And these will go away into everlasting punishment, but the righteous into eternal life." Matthew 25:31, 33, 46

After teaching these four parables, our Lord concludes with a sheep and goats' metaphor. **(Mat. 25:31-46)** Before sitting on the throne of His glory in heaven, the Son will gather at His Coming faithful and unfaithful believers. **(Mat. 25:31, 46)**

He will then begin by separating those practicing evil. **(John 5:28-29)** Before the sheep are rewarded at the Judgment Seat of Christ, the wicked goats will be cast into a furnace of fire where there is wailing and gnashing of teeth. An everlasting fire originally prepared for the Devil and his angels. **(Mat. 25:41)**

"Do not marvel at this; for the hour is coming in which all who are in the graves will hear His voice and come forth—those who have done good, to the resurrection of life, and those who have done evil, to the resurrection of condemnation." John 5:28-29

Jesus taught John there will be a resurrection of those who did evil. At the Coming of the Son of Man, some believers will receive eternal life, while others will be resurrected unto condemnation. **(John 5:28-29)** Sadly, most pastors today are rejecting the timing of this sobering revelation! **(Dan. 12:2)** Instead, some are teaching Jesus will separate the goats from His sheep at the battle of Armageddon. **(Rev. 16:14-16; 19:11-21)** While others vainly insist this separation can only happen at the Great White Throne Judgment. **(Rev. 20:11-15)** Yet, Jesus taught His Coming with be like the days of Noah. **(Mat. 24:37-39)** The Son of Man will gather His elect to heaven **before** pouring out His wrath on the wicked. **(Mark 13:24-27, Luke 17:26-30)** Clearly, Jesus will separate the goats while in heaven. **(Mat. 25:31)** In other words, the Lamb of God won't be sitting on the earth while His wrath is destroying sinners during the Day of The Lord. **(Isa. 13:9-11)** After the Holy Spirit revealed this to me, I was stunned! To be clear, anyone denying this truth is taking away the timing and the consequences of The Son of Man. **(Mat. 24:25)**

"...The Son of Man will send out His angels, and they will gather out of His kingdom all things that offend, and those who practice lawlessness, and will cast them into the furnace of fire. There will be wailing and gnashing of teeth. Then the righteous will shine forth as the sun in the kingdom of their Father. He who has ears to hear, let him hear!"
Matthew 13:41-43

At His Coming, the Son of Man will send forth His angels to gather out of His kingdom all practicing lawlessness. This is the resurrection of believers that did evil. **(John 5:28-29)** Before the sheep are rewarded for their works **(Mat. 16:27)**, the wicked goats will be cast into everlasting fire. **(Mat. 25:41)** The same time the righteous will shine forth in the kingdom of their Father! **(Mat. 13:41-43)** This isn't the wicked that were never saved. They will be judged at the Great White Throne Judgment before being cast into the lake of fire. **(Rev. 20:11-15)**

<u>Who is involved?</u>

"When the Son of Man comes in His glory, and all the holy angels with Him, then He will sit on the throne of His glory. All the nations will be gathered before Him, and He will separate them one from another, as a shepherd divides his sheep from the goats." Matthew 25:31-32

After His Coming, the Son of Man will sit on the throne of His glory in heaven. **(Mat. 25:31-32)** The believers gathered from the nations will be before Him. He will begin by separating the wicked goats from His faithful sheep! After these apostates are cast into everlasting fire, the saints will be rewarded according to their works at the Judgment Seat of Christ. **(Mat. 16:27, 2 Cor. 5:10-11, Rev. 11:18)** After this, they will be married to the Lamb of God. **(Rev. 19:7)**

When will it happen?

"He who sows the good seed is the Son of Man. The field is the world, the good seeds are the sons of the kingdom, but the tares are the sons of the wicked one. The enemy who sowed them is the devil, the harvest is the end of the age, and the reapers are the angels. Therefore, as the tares are gathered and burned in the fire, so it will be at the end of this age." Matthew 13:37-40

During his earthly ministry, Jesus taught his disciples the parable of the tares! This story represents the harvest of believers by the Son of Man. At first, His disciples didn't understand. So, Jesus gave them the literal interpretation. The field is the world. The good seed are the sons of the kingdom. The tares are the sons of the wicked one. The angels will be the reapers at the harvest. **(Mat. 13:37-40)**

'Of how much worse punishment, do you suppose, will he be thought worthy who has trampled the Son of God underfoot, counted the blood of the covenant by which he was sanctified a common thing, and insulted the Spirit of grace? For we know Him who said, "Vengeance is Mine, I will repay," says the Lord. And again, "The LORD will judge His people." It is a fearful thing to fall into the hands of the living God.' Hebrews 10:28-31

The tares were once sanctified by the blood of Jesus. **(Heb. 10:26-31)** After receiving the knowledge of the truth, they chose to willfully sin against their Lord in three ways. One, they trampled the Son of God underfoot. Two, they counted the blood of the covenant a common thing that sanctified them. Three, they insulted the Spirit of Grace! Even so, God will allow them to grow together with the wheat till the harvest. **(Mat. 13:39-42)** After His Coming, these apostates will never again put the Son of God to open shame! Our Lord will repay them with vengeance. It is a fearful thing to fall into the hands of the living God. **(Heb. 10:28-31)**

"Then the king said to the servants, "Bind him hand and foot, take him away, and cast him into outer darkness; there will be weeping and gnashing of teeth." Matthew 22:13

During His ministry, Jesus shared this parable with the chief priests and pharisees. **(Mat. 22:1-13)** The kingdom of heaven is like a king arranging a marriage for his son. While the king visits his guests, he finds someone without a wedding garment. This man was once a son of the kingdom. **(Mat. 8:11-12)** The king orders this person to be cast into outer darkness. What event is Jesus describing in this story? This is the wicked going away to everlasting punishment, while the righteous enter into eternal life. **(Mat. 25:41-46)** And when will this happen during the Second Coming of Christ? Only after the Coming of The Son of Man! **(Mat. 13:39-42)**

How will it happen?

'And many of those who sleep in the dust of the earth shall awake, Some to everlasting life, Some to shame and everlasting contempt.' Daniel 12:2

Daniel also taught a resurrection of dead believers unto condemnation. At the Coming of the Son of Man, some will awake to everlasting life. **(John 5:28-29)** While others will suffer shame and everlasting contempt. **(Dan. 12:2)** Which means this is referring to former believers; not the wicked that were never saved.

"And I say to you that many will come from east and west, and sit down with Abraham, Isaac, and Jacob in the kingdom of heaven. But the sons of the kingdom will be cast out into outer darkness. There will be weeping and gnashing of teeth."
Matthew 8:11-12

There is a day coming when many will sit down in the kingdom of heaven with Abraham, Isaac, and Jacob. **(Mat. 8:11-12)** This will also be the time when the sons of the kingdom practicing iniquity will be cast into outer darkness. **(Mat. 13:39-51)** So when will this happen? The only day the living and the dead will be judged is at the Coming of The Son of Man. **(2 Tim. 4:1, Mark 13:24-27, John 5:28-29)**

Why will it matter?

'For the time has come for judgment to begin at the house of God; and if it begins with us first, what will be the end of those who do not obey the gospel of God?' 1 Peter 3:17

So why will the house of God be judged during the **70th Week**? **(1 Pet. 3:17)** The apostates no longer obeying the gospel will be cast into everlasting fire. **(Mat. 25:41)** While the Son is confessing the names of overcomers to His Father! **(Rev. 3:5)**

"But, Paul, how will apostates ever be gathered to heaven?"

There is only one resurrection of believers at the Coming of The Son of Man. **(Mark 13:26-27, 1 Thes. 4:15-17)** Anyone teaching the resurrection in Matthew 24 is a different resurrection than in Matthew 25 is deceiving the body of Christ. **(Mat. 24:29-39; 25:31-46)** At His Coming, BOTH sheep and goats will be gathered before the throne of God. He who has ears to hear, let him understand!

"Not everyone who says to Me, 'Lord, Lord,' shall enter the kingdom of heaven, but he who does the will of My Father in heaven. Many will say to Me in that day, 'Lord, Lord, have we not prophesied in Your name, cast out demons in Your name, and done many wonders in Your name?' And then I will declare to them, 'I never knew you; depart from Me, you who practice lawlessness!' Matthew 7:21-23

Not everyone who says, 'Lord, Lord,' shall enter the kingdom of heaven. **(Mat. 7:21-23)** Only those who do the will of their Father will receive incorruptible bodies. **(1 Cor. 15:50-52)** On the last day, many professing Christ will be crying out, *'Lord, Lord.'* They will confess the many wonders they did in His Name. How they prophesied and cast out demons in His Name. Sadly, the good works they're declaring took place when they were saved! Then why did Jesus declare He never knew them? 'Knew' represents the intimacy between a man and a woman. Jesus never intimately knew the believer's practicing lawlessness. When they stand before the Son of Man, they are no longer saved! **(Luke 21:36, Heb. 10:26-30)** Tragically, they will go away to everlasting punishment. **(Mat. 25:46, Jude 1:4)**

'And now, little children, abide in Him, that when He appears, we may have confidence and not be ashamed before Him at His coming.' 1 John 2:28

Who will have confidence during The Feast of Trumpets? **(Mat. 24:30-36)** It will be the overcomers gloriously redeemed by the Son of Man. **(Mark 13:24-27)** And who will be ashamed at His Coming? **(1 John 2:28)** It will be the transgressors no longer abiding in Christ! **(Mat. 25:41, 2 John 1:9-10)** They will never again experience the presence of the Father, the Son, and the Holy Spirit! **(Heb. 6:4-6, 1 John 5:7)** My brethren, how can anyone understand the Second Coming without understanding this critical revelation? **(Mat. 25:31-46)** May the Holy Spirit bear witness! **(John 14:26)** There will be a resurrection of righteous and unrighteous at His Coming. **(John 5:28-29, Dan. 12:2)**

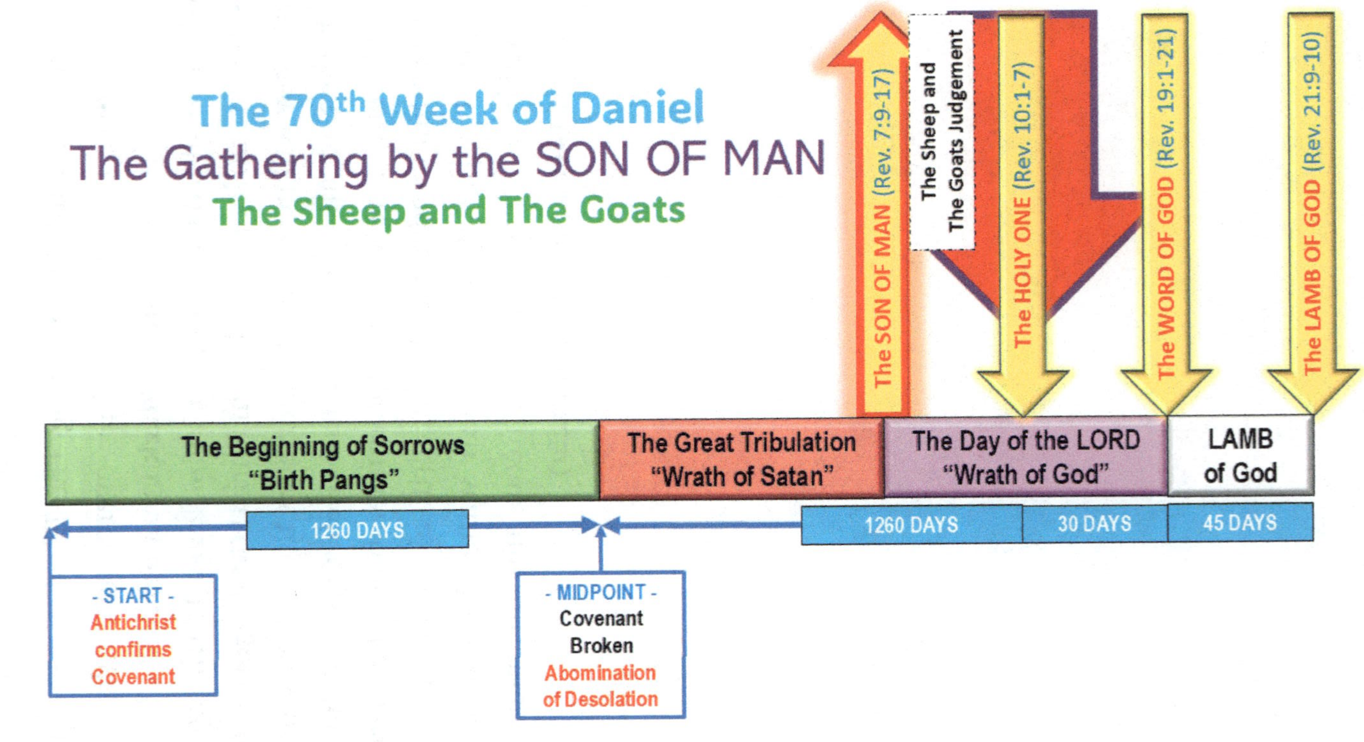

The 70th Week of Daniel
The Gathering by the SON OF MAN
The Sheep and The Goats
The SON OF MAN (Rev. 7:9-17)
The Sheep and The Goats Judgement
The HOLY ONE (Rev. 10:1-7)
The WORD OF GOD (Rev. 19:1-21)
The LAMB OF GOD (Rev. 21:9-10)
The Beginning of Sorrows
"Birth Pangs"
The Great Tribulation
"Wrath of Satan"
The Day of the LORD
"Wrath of God"
LAMB
of God
1260 DAYS
1260 DAYS
30 DAYS
45 DAYS
- START -
Antichrist
confirms
Covenant
- MIDPOINT -
Covenant
Broken
Abomination
of Desolation

17

Seventh Seal: Silence in Heaven

'..."Do not weep. Behold, the Lion of the tribe of Judah, the Root of David, has prevailed to open the scroll and to loose its seven seals." Revelation 5:5

John must have composed himself. Nothing could duplicate the sign of The Day of The Lord! **(Isa. 13:9-11)** He watched the constellations lose their light during the Feast of Trumpets. **(1 Cor. 15:52, Rev. 6:12-17)** Just like Jesus foretold. **(Mat. 24:25, 29, 36)** It must have felt like eternity before John saw the sign of the Son of Man. **(Mat. 24:30)** The saints from heaven are coming back with Jesus. **(1 Thes. 4:13-16, Jude 1:14)** At the last trump, a great multitude of overcomers will come out of the Great Tribulation and stand before the throne of God. **(1 Thes. 4:17, Rev. 7:9-17, Mat. 25:31)** A solemn John knew what was coming. **(John 6:44)** The same day resurrected believers begin worshiping the Father and the Lamb in heaven **(Mat. 25:31)**, fire will begin burning the wicked left behind! **(Rev. 6:16-17; 8:1-5)**

What is this event?

'When He opened the seventh seal, there was silence in heaven for about half an hour.' Revelation 8:1

John watched as the Lamb opened the **Seventh Seal**. **(Rev. 8:1)** For about half an hour, there was silence in heaven. Why such a solemn time? After this silence ends, God Almighty will punish the world for its evil and the wicked for their iniquity. During the Day of The Lord, the wrath of the Lamb will lay the earth desolate! **(Isa. 13:9-11, Rev. 6:16-17; 15:2)**

'And I saw the seven angels who stand before God, and to them were given seven trumpets. Then another angel, having a golden censer, came and stood at the altar. He was given much incense, that he should offer it with the prayers of all the saints upon the golden altar which was before the throne. And the smoke of the incense, with the prayers of the saints, ascended before God from the angel's hand.' Revelation 8:2-4

After the silence in heaven ended, John saw seven angels standing ready. Each was given a trumpet to sound. Then another angel holding a censor stood before the golden altar. He was given incense to offer with the prayers of the saints in heaven. Instantly, the smoke of the incense ascended from the angel's hand! **(Rev. 8:1-4)**

'Then the angel took the censer, filled it with fire from the altar, and threw it to the earth. And there were noises thunderings, lightnings, and an earthquake.' Revelation 8:5

Then the angel took the golden censer from the altar. **(Rev. 8:5)** He filled it with fire before throwing it to earth! Thunders, lightings and an earthquake will be felt by the wicked left behind. This is the beginning of the Day of The Lord! **(Isa. 13:6)**

Who is involved?

'And said to the mountains and rocks, "Fall on us and hide us from the face of Him who sits on the throne and from the wrath of the Lamb! For the great day of His wrath has come, and who is able to stand?' Revelation 6:16-17

The wicked will be living in peace and safety during the Great Tribulation. **(1 Thes. 5:3, Luke 17:26-30, Mat. 24:37-39)** Until the day the earth begins to burn with fire. **(Rev. 8:1-5)** The massive hysteria will be unbearable! The wrath of the Lamb is coming and no one has the power to stop it! All having the mark of the Beast will hide from the face of Him who sits on the throne! **(Rev. 6:16-17)**

'And to wait for His Son from heaven, whom He raised from the dead, even Jesus who delivers us from the wrath to come.' 1 Thessalonians 1:10

Due to widespread apostasy, everyone having the testimony of Jesus will experience Satan's great wrath during the Great Tribulation. **(Mat. 24:9-29, Rev. 7:9-17; 12:12)** This horrific persecution will begin the second half of the **70th Week**, the same day the Lamb opens the **Fourth Seal**. **(Mat. 24:15, Rev. 6:7-8)** After the **Sixth Seal**, the heavens will lose their light during the Great Tribulation. **(Mat. 24:29, Rev. 6:12-17)** Amidst this darkness, overcomers from every nation will be caught up before the throne of God. **(1 Thes. 1:10, Rev. 7:9-17)** This is the promise by Jesus to deliver us from the wrath to come. **(John 14:1-4, Mat. 24:13)**

'Then I saw another sign in heaven, great and marvelous: seven angels having the seven last plagues, for in them the wrath of God is complete.' Revelation 15:1

On this same day, the Lamb will open the **Seventh Seal**. **(Rev. 8:1)** After a half an hour of silence in heaven, angels will sound seven trumpets. **(Rev. 8:1-2)** After the death and destruction from these trumpets ends, all having the mark of the beast will suffer God's final wrath, the last seven plagues (bowls). **(Rev. 15:1; 16:1-21)**

<u>When will it happen?</u>

'Looking for and hastening the coming of the day of God, because of which the heavens will be dissolved, being on fire, and the elements will melt with fervent heat? 2 Peter 3:12

Although rarely taught, the wrath of the Lamb will erupt after the opening of the **Seventh Seal**. **(Rev. 6:16-17; 8:1-8)** The day the heavens dissolve, the earth will melt with fervent heat. Isaiah calls it the Day of The Lord. **(Isa. 13:9)** Paul calls it the Day of Christ. **(2 Thes. 2:2)** Peter calls it, the coming day of God. **(2 Pet. 3:12)**

"No one can come to Me unless the Father who sent Me draws him; and I will raise him up at the last day." John 6:40

Between the **Sixth** and **Seventh Seals,** John saw three events take place on the last day. Jesus will cut short the Great Tribulation by delivering alive believers to heaven, before pouring out His wrath on the wicked left behind! **(John 6:40)**

<u>How will it happen</u>?

'Finally, there is laid up for me the crown of righteousness, which the Lord, the righteous Judge, will give to me on that Day, and not to me only but also to all who have loved His appearing.'
2 Timothy 4:8

Today, many are vainly teaching God is going to shorten the **70th Week** of Daniel! Brethren, how is this premise taking away the timing and consequences of the Most Holy? **(Dan. 9:24)** Satan will give his authority over the nations to the Beast for 1,260 days, the entire second half of the **70th Week. (Rev. 13:3-7)** The Two Witnesses will also prophesy the second half of the **70th Week**. **(Rev. 11:3)** The Most Holy will fulfill the mystery of God the day after the **70th Week** is completed. **(Dan. 9:24, Heb. 9:28, Rev. 10:1-7)** On this same day, five days before the sounding of the **Seventh Trumpet,** the Beast will kill the Two Witnesses. **(Rev. 11:7)** Which means the second half of the **70th Week** will end between the **Sixth** and **Seventh Trumpets**. **(Rev. 10:1-7; 11:15)** For the sake of His elect, the Lamb will cut short the Great Tribulation after opening the **Sixth Seal**. **(Mat. 24:21-22, 29-31)** The **70th Week** of Daniel prophecy will never be cut short! **(Dan. 9:24)**

Why will it matter?

'And for this reason God will send them strong delusion, that they should believe the lie, that they all may be condemned who did not believe the truth but had pleasure in unrighteousness.'
2 Thessalonians 2:11-12

Thirty minutes after the **Seventh Seal** is opened, all having the mark of the Beast will be under the influence of a strong delusion from God. **(2 Thes. 2:11)** Instead of receiving the love of the truth during the Great Tribulation, they will choose to obey the Lawless One. **(2 Thes. 2:3-4)** There is no forgiveness for those controlled by this delusion. **(Rev. 14:9-11)** All taking pleasure in unrighteousness, will condemn themselves for eternity. **(2 Thes. 2:12)**

"...Do not harm the earth, the sea, or the trees till we have sealed the servants of our God on their foreheads." And I heard the number of those who were sealed. One hundred and forty-four thousand of all the tribes of the children of Israel were sealed." Revelation 7:3-4

The 144,000 from Israel will receive the seal of God before the opening of the **Seventh Seal**. **(Rev. 7:1-8; 8:1)** They will later be physically saved from the protected remnant in the wilderness. **(Rev. 12:6, Zech. 13:8-9)** If they were spiritually saved before the resurrection, they also would have been caught up to heaven. Yet, John sees the Lamb and the 144,000 standing on Mount Zion during the future Feast of Tabernacles. **(Rev. 11:15; 14:1-4, 14-16)**

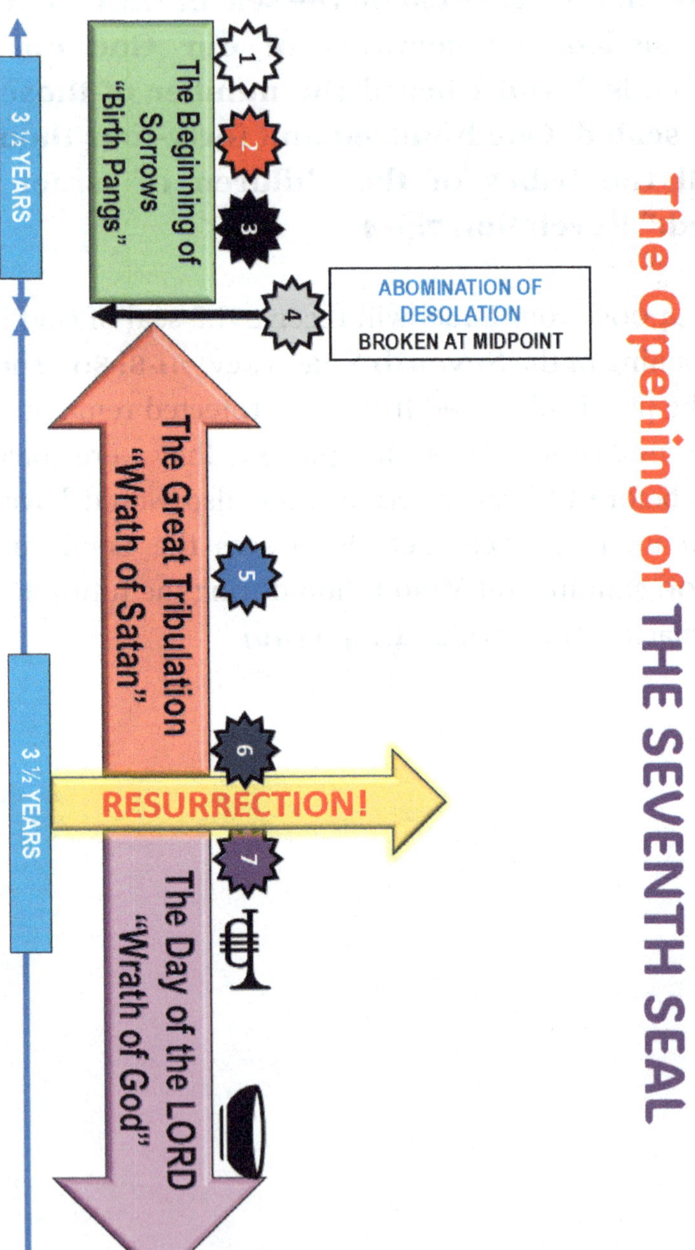
The Opening of THE SEVENTH SEAL
ABOMINATION OF DESOLATION
BROKEN AT MIDPOINT
The Beginning of Sorrows "Birth Pangs"
The Great Tribulation "Wrath of Satan"
RESURRECTION!
The Day of the LORD "Wrath of God"
3 ½ YEARS
3 ½ YEARS
1
2
3
4
5
6
7

18

Day of The Lord: Wrath of The Lamb

"... Fall on us and hide us from the face of Him who sits on the throne and from the wrath of the Lamb. For the great day of His wrath has come, and who is able to stand?" Revelation 6:16-17

Why should everyone understand the difference between the wrath of Satan and the wrath of the Lamb during the second half of the **70th Week**? **(Mat. 24:15, Rev. 12:12; 6:16-17)** It's because the offering of peace and safety by the Beast during the Great Tribulation will have an eternal price tag! **(Rev. 13:11-18; 14:9-11)** After overcomers from every nation are delivered by our great God and Savior **(Titus 2:13, Mark 13:26-27, Rev. 7:9-17)**, Satan's wrath during the Great Tribulation will be replaced by Gods wrath during the Day of The Lord! **(Rev. 6:16-17; 8:2; 15:1)**

'Therefore rejoice, O heavens, and you who dwell in them! Woe to the inhabitants of the earth and the sea! For the devil has come down to you, having great wrath, because he knows that he has a short time.' Revelation 12:12

"But, Paul, most don't believe this! How can anyone understand the differences between the Great Tribulation and the Day of The Lord?"

My friends, by sharing this biblical sequence of events!
"During the Great Tribulation, every eye will see the Son coming back in the glory of His Father. At the trump of God, angels will gather overcomers from Satan's great wrath. They will receive incorruptible bodies before praising the Father and the Son for their salvation. After a half an hour of silence in heaven, the great day of God's wrath, the Day of The Lord, will begin melting the earth."

What is this event?

'Behold, the day of the LORD comes, Cruel, with both wrath and fierce anger, to lay the land desolate; And He will destroy its sinners from it.' For the stars of heaven and their constellations Will not give their light; The sun will be darkened in its going forth, And the moon will not cause its light to shine. "I will punish the world for its evil, And the wicked for their iniquity; I will halt the arrogance of the proud, and will lay low the haughtiness of the terrible.' Isaiah 13:9-11

The days of the Great Tribulation will end the day the constellations lose their light. **(Mat. 24:29, Rev. 6:12-17)** After believers from heaven and earth are caught up **(Mark 13:24-27, 1 Thes. 4:15-17)**, Jesus will begin by punishing the world for its evil. **(Isa. 13:11)** The wrath of the Lamb will be destroying sinners left behind. **(Rev. 6:16-17; 8:2)** Imagine John's reaction after seeing the sign of The Son of Man on the same day. **(Mat. 24:29-30)** So why is Satan hiding this truth? Only the overcomers seeing these two signs will stand before the Son of Man. **(Luke 21:36)**

'So I looked, and behold, a pale horse. And the name of him who sat on it was Death, and Hades followed with him. And power was given to them over a fourth of the earth, to kill with sword, with hunger, with death, and by the beasts of the earth.' Revelation 6:8

In his vision, John saw this sequence of events! **(Rev. 1:1-3)** The Great Tribulation will erupt the same day the Lamb opens the **Fourth Seal**. **(Rev. 6:7-8)** Death and Hades will come down having the power to kill over a fourth of the earth. **(Mat. 24:9-26)** On this same day, Satan will grant his power over the nations to the Beast. **(Rev. 12:12; 13:1-5)** Clearly, the events of the Great Tribulation are never called God's wrath! After the opening of the **Sixth Seal**, every believer will be caught up before the throne of God in heaven. **(Rev. 6:12-17; 7:9-17)** On this same day, John saw the Lamb opening the **Seventh Seal**! **(Rev. 8:1)** After a half an hour of silence in heaven, an angel will cast a censer full of fire to earth. **(Rev. 8:3-5)** Sadly, most Christians are rejecting the timing of this revelation. This is why so many living during the Great Tribulation **(Mat. 24:15-22),** will have no idea when the wrath of the Lamb will erupt during the **70th Week**! **(Rev. 8:1-5)**

Who is involved?

"Woe to you who desire the day of the Lord! For what good is the day of the Lord to you? It will be darkness, and not light." Amos 5:18

The Day of The Lord is divided into two halves. **(Isa. 13:9-11, Amos 5:18)** John saw the events from the **Seven Trumpets** **(Rev. 8-9; 11:15-18)**, followed by the events from the **Seven Bowls**. **(Rev. 16:1-21)** Gods final wrath will end after the **Seventh Bowl** is poured out on the followers of the Beast. **(Rev. 15:1; 16:17)** Make no mistake, His wrath upon sinners won't begin until every overcomer is gathered before the throne of His glory. **(Mat. 25:31, Luke 21:36)**

"Then Death and Hades were cast into the lake of fire. This is the second death. And anyone not found written in the Book of Life was cast into the lake of fire." Revelation 20:14-15

After the **Seventh Bowl** is poured out **(Rev. 16:17-21)**, Jesus will begin killing everyone having the mark of the beast at the supper of the great God! **(Rev. 14:9-11; 19:11-21)** Their suffering will begin in Hades. At the Great White Throne, the wicked will be resurrected out of Hades. Jesus will then pronounce a final judgment before casting them into the Lake of Fire. **(Rev. 20:11-15)**

"And this is the will of Him who sent Me, that everyone who sees the Son and believes in Him may have everlasting life; and I will raise him up at the last day." John 6:40

All believers will receive everlasting life on the last day! **(John 6:40)** The apostle Paul calls the last day, the day of Christ **(2 Thes. 2:2)**, the day of The Lord Jesus Christ **(1 Cor. 1:8)**, the day of The Lord Jesus **(1 Cor. 5:5)**, and the day of Jesus Christ. **(Phil. 1:6)** On this day, the Son will raise up His elect before pouring out His wrath on the wicked left behind. **(Mat. 24:29-39, Mark 13:24-27, Luke 21:24-28)**

When will it happen?

"But this is the covenant that I will make with the house of Israel after those days, says the Lord**: I will put My law in their minds, and write it on their hearts; and I will be their God, and they shall be My people... For I will forgive their iniquity, and their sin I will remember no more." Jeremiah 31:33-34**

"And so all Israel will be saved, as it is written: The Deliverer will come out of Zion, And He will turn away ungodliness from Jacob; For this is My covenant with them, when I take away their sins." Romans 11:26-27

During the Day of The Lord, when will the Deliverer make a new covenant with the house of Israel? **(Rom. 11:25-27)** So what will happen to the Jewish people after Jesus fulfills the Feast of Trumpets? **(Mark 13:24-27, 1 Cor. 15:51-52, Rev. 7:9-17)** Miraculously, the Most Holy will take away their sins on the Day of Atonement. **(Dan. 9:24, Rev. 10:1-7)** According to the will of God, one third of Israel will be spiritually and physically saved. **(Zech. 13:8-9)** During the Feast of Tabernacles **(Rev. 14:1-4; 14-16)**, the Lamb will declare, *"This is my people."* This final ingathering of born-again Jews will reply, *"The LORD is my God."* **(Jer. 31:31-34)**

'Since it is a righteous thing with God to repay with tribulation those who trouble you, and to give you who are troubled rest with us when the Lord Jesus is revealed from heaven with His mighty angels, in flaming fire taking vengeance on those who do not know God, and on those who do not obey the gospel of our Lord Jesus Christ.' 2 Thessalonians 1:6-8

Many ask, when will the Lord Jesus be revealed with His mighty angels? The Lamb will begin by repaying all who troubled His future wife! **(Rev. 19:7)** For those not knowing

God, Jesus will repay in flaming fire! **(Isa. 13:9-11, Rev. 8:1-5)** For the believers not obeying the gospel, they will also suffer His vengeance. In God's eyes, there is no difference between the two! **(2 Thes. 1:6-8)**

"Let the nations be wakened, and come up to the Valley of Jehoshaphat; For there I will sit to judge all the surrounding nations. Put in the sickle, for the harvest is ripe. Come, go down; For the winepress is full, The vats overflow. For their wickedness is great." Multitudes, multitudes in the valley of decision! For the day of the LORD is near in the valley of decision. The sun and moon will grow dark, And the stars will diminish their brightness The LORD also will roar from Zion, And utter His voice from Jerusalem; The heavens and earth will shake; But the LORD will be a shelter for His people, And the strength of the children of Israel." Joel 3:12-16

The time has come for the Lord to sit in judgment of the wicked nations surrounding Israel. **(Joel 3:12-16)** From the north is Lebanon and Syria, from the east is Jordan, from the south is Egypt. There are eighteen more Islamic régimes vowing to destroy the children of Israel. Their shedding of innocent blood has grown during the **70th Week. (Joel 3:13, 19)** Just days before the sun, moon, and stars grow dark **(Joel 3:15, Mat. 24:29, Rev. 6:12-17)** God will draw multitudes into the Valley of Jehoshaphat. **(Joel 3:12)** Their wickedness will be judged in the valley of decision. So why will the overcomers living during the Great Tribulation be rejoicing after witnessing this righteous judgment? **(Rev. 7:9-17)** They will know the Day of The Lord is near. **(Joel 3:14, Isa. 13:9-11, 2 Thes. 2:1-4)**

"But of that day and hour no one knows, not even the angels of heaven, but My Father only.' Matthew 24:36

"But, Paul, Jesus said no one knows the day or hour of His Coming! Which means The Day of The Lord can take place at any moment!" (False)

The honoring of the Feast of Trumpets takes place every new year after the spotting of a new moon. In some years, due to heavy clouds, it takes two days to identify the new moon. This is why no one will know when this Feast begins! **(Mat. 24:36)** Clearly, Jesus will fulfill this holy Feast at the last trump. **(1 Cor. 15:52)** After the constellations lose their light, the sign of the Day of The Lord. **(Isa. 13:9-11, Mark 13:24-27)**

How will it happen?

"Fall on us and hide us from the face of Him who sits on the throne and from the wrath of the Lamb! For the great day of His wrath has come, and who is able to stand?" Revelation 6:16-17

How are Christians taking away the consequences of The Day of The Lord? By believing the Great Tribulation is God's wrath. Sadly, they just can't see the reason for Satan's great wrath during the **Fourth** and **Fifth Seals**. **(Rev. 6:7-11)** The purpose of the Great Tribulation is to test the faith of all having the testimony of Jesus. **(Rev. 12:12-17)** The purpose of the Day of The Lord is to punish the world for its evil. **(Isa. 13:9-11, Rev. 8:2; 15:1)** By quoting Daniel, Jesus places each in the second half of the **70th Week**. **(Mat. 24:15-22, 37-39)**

'And the smoke of the incense, with the prayers of the saints, ascended before God from the angel's hand. Then the angel took the censer, filled it with fire from the altar, and threw it to the earth. And there were noises, thunderings, lightnings, and an earthquake.' Revelation 8:4-5

Three events will take place on the day God's wrath is poured out!

(1) The constellations will lose their light. **(Acts 2:20, Mat. 24:29, Rev. 6:12-17)**

(2) A great multitude of believers will be gathered out of the Great Tribulation before the throne of God in heaven. **(Rev. 7:9-17)**

(3) The followers of the Beast will suffer the wrath of the Lamb during the Day of The Lord! **(Rev. 8:1-5; 15:1; 16:1-21)**

‘Not forsaking the assembling of ourselves together, as is the manner of some, but exhorting one another, and so much the more as you see the Day approaching.’ Hebrews 10:25

**“For whoever is ashamed of Me and My words in this adulterous and sinful generation, of him the Son of Man also will be ashamed when He comes in the glory of His Father with the holy angels.”
Mark 8:38**

Paul is exhorting us not to forsake our assembling together as we see the Day of The Lord approaching. **(Heb. 10:25)** It’s because a fearful expectation of judgment during the Great Tribulation is awaiting those ashamed of Jesus. **(Mark 8:38)** After the heavens go dark, every overcomer will be looking up for their physical redemption. **(Luke 21:25-28)**

‘And I saw the seven angels who stand before God, and to them were given seven trumpets...So the seven angels who had the seven trumpets prepared themselves to sound.’ Revelation 8:2, 6

John witnessed the judgments from the future **Seven Trumpets**. **(Rev. 8:2)**The unimaginable suffering of sinners by a Holy God! **(Isa. 13:9-11)**

First Trumpet: The grass on earth will burn up. **(Rev. 8:7)**
Second Trumpet: A third of the sea will turn blood red. **(Rev. 8:9)**
Third Trumpet: Sinners drinking infected water will die. **(Rev. 8:10-11)**
Fourth Trumpet: A third of the day will not shine. **(Rev. 8:12-13)**
Fifth Trumpet: Many would rather die than continue to suffer! **(Rev. 9:1-12)**

'By these three plagues a third of mankind was killed—by the fire and the smoke and the brimstone which came out of their mouths.' Revelation 9:18

After the **Sixth Trumpet**, four demons will kill a third of mankind. **(Rev. 9:13-18)** They will kill by fire, smoke and brimstone coming from their mouths. Even after suffering the horrific torment from these plagues, the surviving wicked will refuse to repent of their murders, sorceries, sexual immorality, and thefts! **(Rev. 9:20-21)**

'Now when He had spoken these things, while they watched, He was taken up, and a cloud received Him out of their sight. And while they looked steadfastly toward heaven as He went up, behold, two men stood by them in white apparel, who also said, "Men of Galilee, why do you stand gazing up into heaven? This same Jesus, who was taken up from you into heaven, will so come in like manner as you saw Him go into heaven." Acts 1:9-11

The **70th Week** will end after the sounding of the **Sixth Trumpet**. On this day, the Holy One will return on the Day of Atonement. **(Dan. 9:24)** Clothed in a cloud, He will put one foot on the sea and one foot on the land. **(Rev. 10:1-7, Acts 1:9-11)**

On the first day, the Christ will fulfill the mystery of God. **(Rev. 10:1-7)**
On the second day, Micah sees the King leading His people. **(Mic. 2:13)**
On the third day, Hosea sees the salvation of Israel. **(Hos. 6:1-2)**
On the fourth day, the Two Witnesses will ascend to heaven. **(Rev. 11:11-14)**
On the fifth day, the Lamb of God and the 144,000 from the twelve tribes of Israel will be celebrating the Feast of Tabernacles. **(Rev. 14:1-4, 14-16)**

'Then the seventh angel sounded: And there were loud voices in heaven, saying, "The kingdoms of this world have become the kingdoms of our Lord and of His Christ, and He shall reign forever and ever!" Revelation 11:15

After the Day of Atonement is completed, the Christ will personally fulfill the Feast of Tabernacles! The world will witness this miracle! Everyone will be watching as the Lamb leads the saved 144,000 to the top of Mount Zion. **(Rev. 14:1-4)** This is the final harvest of Jews to Jerusalem. **(Rev. 14:14-16)** Satan understands what this means. On the sixth day, the ruler of this world will be stripped of his power at the sounding of the **Seventh Trumpet**. **(Rev. 11:15)** Loud voices in heaven will announce it. The kingdoms of this world will become the kingdoms of our Lord and of His Christ. Almighty God will begin reigning during the Feast of Tabernacles. **(Lev. 23:1-44)** Before destroying the kingdom of the Beast! **(Rev. 15:1; 16:1-21)**

"And in that day His feet will stand on the Mount of Olives, which faces Jerusalem on the east. And the Mount of Olives shall be split in two...making a very large valley...Then you shall flee through My mountain valley, For the mountain valley shall reach to Azal..." Zechariah 14:4-5

On the sixth day, Jesus will create a shield of protection! He will split the Mount of Olives in two. **(Zech. 14:4-5)** The saved remnant from Israel will flee through this mountain valley to Azal. After safely reaching this refuge, all blaspheming God will suffer the fierceness of His wrath! **(Rev. 15:1; 16:1-21)**

'Then I saw another sign in heaven, great and marvelous: seven angels having the seven last plagues, for in them the wrath of God is complete...Then one of the four living creatures gave to the seven angels seven golden bowls full of the wrath of God who lives forever and ever.' Revelation 15:1, 7

These seven last plagues will demolish this Christ rejecting world. **(Rev. 15:1)**

First Bowl: All having the mark of the Beast will suffer foul sores. **(Rev. 16:1-2)**
Second Bowl: Creatures in the sea will die.
(Rev. 16:3)
Third Bowl: Rivers and lakes will look like blood.
(Rev. 16:4-7)
Fourth Bowl: Sinners will be scorched by the sun.
(Rev. 16:8-9)
Fifth Bowl: Followers of the Beast will blaspheme God.
(Rev. 16:10-11)
Sixth Bowl: Demons will gather armies to Armageddon.
(Rev. 16:12-16)

'Then the seventh angel poured out his bowl into the air, and a loud voice came out of the temple of heaven, from the throne, saying, "It is done!" Revelation 16:17

After the **Seventh Bowl** is poured into the air, great hail will fall on those having the mark of the Beast. **(Rev. 16:17-21)** The pain will be so great the wicked will continue to blaspheme God. Then a loud voice from the temple in heaven will say, *"It is done."* This final bowl will complete the Day of The Lord! **(Rev. 15:1)**

<u>**Why will it matter?**</u>

'For you yourselves know perfectly that the day of the Lord so comes as a thief in the night. For when they say, "Peace and safety," then sudden destruction comes upon them, as labor pains upon a pregnant woman. And they shall not escape.' 1 Thessalonians 5:2-3

The Day of The Lord will come as a thief in the night during the **70th Week**. The Dragon, the Beast, and the False Prophet will be powerless to stop it! **(Rev. 16:13)** So who will be counted worthy to escape the Day of The Lord, the wrath of the Lamb? **(Isa. 13:9-11, Rev. 6:16-17, 1 Thes. 5:2-3)** It will be a great multitude of faithful Christians caught up out of the Great Tribulation. **(Rev. 7:9-17)** The apostates having the mark of the Beast will not escape the wrath of the Lamb. **(Rev. 14:9-11)**

'Now out of His mouth goes a sharp sword, that with it He should strike the nations. And He Himself will rule them with a rod of iron. He Himself treads the winepress of the fierceness and wrath of Almighty God.' Revelation 19:15

After the **Seventh Bowl**, the Word will thread the wrath of God Almighty at the supper of the great God. **(Rev. 19:15-17)** Jesus will begin by casting the Beast and the False Prophet into the lake of fire! Before killing their followers. **(Rev. 19:20-21)**

"And from the time that the daily sacrifice is taken away, and the abomination of desolation is set up, there shall be one thousand two hundred and ninety days." Daniel 12:11

The second half of the **70th Week** is 1,260 days. **(Rev. 11:3)** Thirty days later (1290 days) **(Dan. 12:11)**, Jesus will cast the

Beast into the lake of fire at the great day of God Almighty, Armageddon. **(Dan. 7:11, Rev. 16:14-16; 19:11-21)**

'Blessed is he who waits, and comes to the one thousand three hundred and thirty-five days.' Daniel 12:12

Forty-five days after Armageddon (1335 days) **(Dan. 12:12)**, the Lamb and His wife will come down inside the Holy Jerusalem. **(Rev. 21:9-10)** They will rule over a new earth for a thousand years. **(Rev. 20:6)**

'And the nations of those who are saved shall walk in its light, and the kings of the earth bring their glory and honor into it... And they shall bring the glory and the honor of the nations into it. But there shall by no means enter it anything that defiles, or causes an abomination or a lie, but only those who are written in the Lamb's Book of Life.'
Revelation 21:24, 26-27

During His 1,000 year reign, saved and unsaved people will be living among the nations. **(Rev. 20:6; 21:24-27)** Jesus taught only those whose names are in the Lamb's Book of Life, will be able to bring honor and glory into the holy Jerusalem! After entering the holy city, they will see the Father and His Son. Around their throne will be the glorified wife of the Lamb! **(Rev. 21:9-10)** The surviving wicked will never be able to defile this holy tabernacle hovering over physical Jerusalem! **(Rev. 21:27)** After a thousand years, Satan will be released from his prison. He will begin by gathering the support of the wicked. Their number will be like the sand of the sea. They will go forth and surround Jerusalem, the camp of the saints. Then God will devour them with fire. This will be the final fate of mankind! **(Rev. 20:7-9)**

'Who has performed and done it, Calling the generations from the beginning? 'I, the Lord, am the first; And with the last I am He.' Isaiah 41:4

This means Jesus, the First and the Last, will save believers from every generation. **(Isa. 41:4, Rev. 22:13)** This includes the faithful before **(Rev. 7:9-17)**, during **(Rev. 10:7)** and after the Day of The Lord. **(Rev. 21:24-26)**

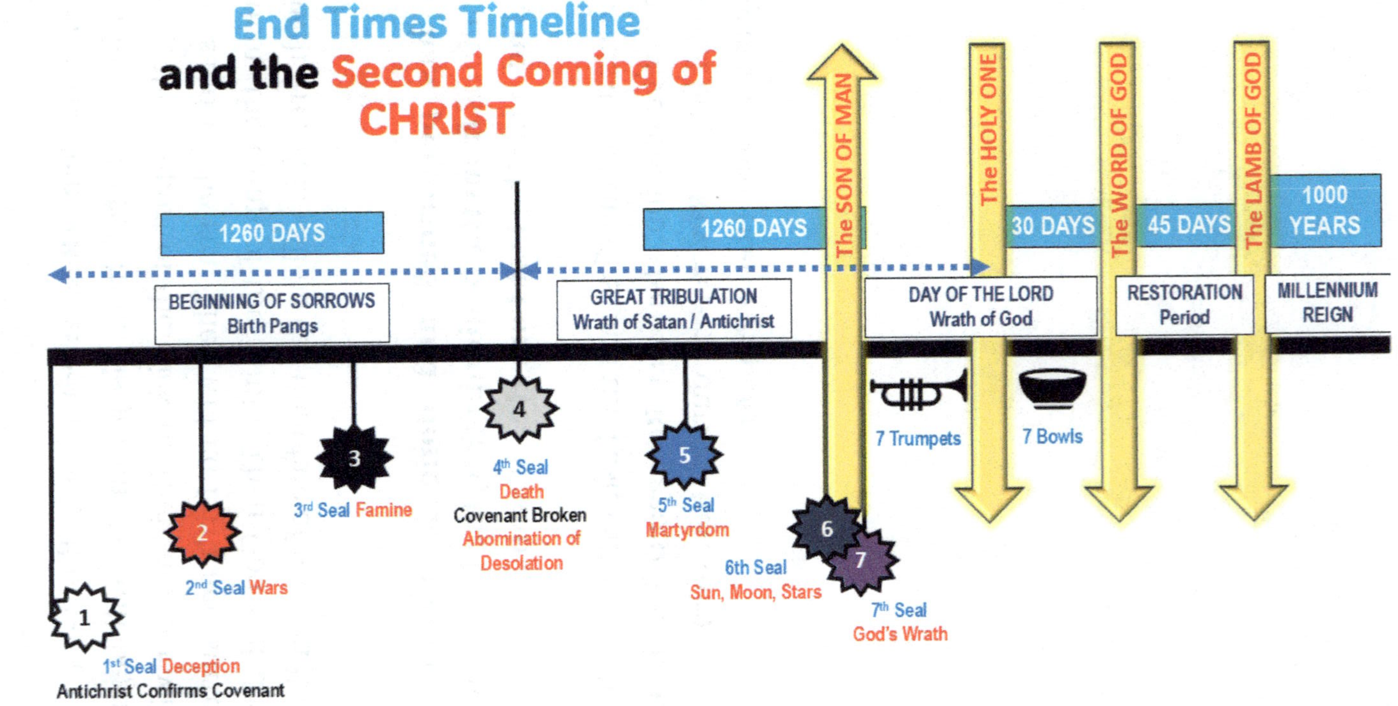
End Times Timeline
and the Second Coming of
CHRIST
1260 DAYS
BEGINNING OF SORROWS
Birth Pangs
1260 DAYS
GREAT TRIBULATION
Wrath of Satan / Antichrist
The SON OF MAN
The HOLY ONE
30 DAYS
DAY OF THE LORD
Wrath of God
The WORD OF GOD
45 DAYS
RESTORATION
Period
The LAMB OF GOD
1000
YEARS
MILLENNIUM
REIGN
1st Seal Deception
Antichrist Confirms Covenant
2nd Seal Wars
3rd Seal Famine
4th Seal
Death
Covenant Broken
Abomination of
Desolation
5th Seal
Martyrdom
6th Seal
Sun, Moon, Stars
7th Seal
God's Wrath
7 Trumpets
7 Bowls

19

Final Warning: The Book of Life

"And if anyone takes away from the words of the book of this prophecy, God shall take away his part from the Book of Life, from the holy city, and from the things which are written in this book." Revelation 22:19

John was by His side throughout His entire ministry. **(John 13:23)** Imagine, Jesus taught His close friend the actual pillars of the doctrine of Christ! Those continually abiding in these divine truths have both the Father and the Son! **(2 John 1:9-11)**

The Gospel!
"For God so loved the world that He gave His only begotten Son, that whoever believes in Him should not perish but have everlasting life." John 3:16

The Virgin Birth!
"And the Word became flesh and dwelt among us, and we beheld His glory, the glory as of the only begotten of the Father, full of grace and truth." John 1:14

The Triune Nature of God!
"For there are three that bear witness in heaven: the Father, the Word, and the Holy Spirit; and these three are one." 1 John 5:7

The Holy Spirit!
"But the Helper, the Holy Spirit, whom the Father will send in My name, He will teach you all things, and bring to your remembrance all things that I said to you." John 14:26

The Feasts of The Lord!
"On the last day, that great day of the feast, Jesus stood and cried out, saying, "If anyone thirsts, let him come to Me and drink." John 7:37

The Coming of The Lord!
"In My Father's house are many mansions; if it were not so, I would have told you. I go to prepare a place for you. And if I go and prepare a place for you, I will come again and receive you to Myself; that where I am, there you may be also." John 14:2-3

<u>The Resurrection unto Life and Condemnation!</u>

"Do not marvel at this; for the hour is coming in which all who are in the graves will hear His voice and come forth—those who have done good, to the resurrection of life, and those who have done evil, to the resurrection of condemnation." John 5:28-29

<u>The Lake of Fire!</u>

"If anyone does not abide in Me, he is cast out as a branch and is withered; and they gather them and throw them into the fire, and they are burned." John 15:6

The time was March 22, 1975. It was the night I asked Jesus to forgive me of my sins. Receiving the indwelling of the Holy Spirit was a miracle! **(John 20:22)** The peace I received after believing in His death, burial, and resurrection was hard to describe. **(1 Cor. 15:1-4)** I was born again into the kingdom of our Lord and Savior Jesus Christ. **(2 Pet. 2:11)** In my first year serving the Lord, I learned the above pillars of the doctrine of Christ! The witness from the Holy Spirit was so powerful. I had no doubt I would continually abide in Christ. Yet, in the next fifty years, I have witnessed more and more Christians denying these divine truths. And who is carrying out these evil attacks? Here are three examples of believers transgressing the doctrine of Christ!

‘Whoever transgresses and does not abide in the doctrine of Christ does not have God. He who abides in the doctrine of Christ has both the Father and the Son.’ 2 John 1:9

(1) *Denial of the Virgin Birth*

I remember hearing a pastor from a mega church in America denying the Virgin Birth! It was a stunning departure from the faith. **(John 1:14)**

(2) *Denial of The Godhead*

There is one Godhead. Consisting of the Father, the Son and the Holy Spirit! **(1 John 5:7)** The lie the Son is somehow the Father is a doctrine of demons! **(1 Tim. 4:1)** Refusing to believe in the triune nature of God is heretical. **(John 14:26)**

(3) *Denial of the Promise of The Father*

Taking away the hope of ever receiving the Promise of the Father, the baptism of the Holy Spirit, is from Satan. **(Acts 1:4-5)** Anyone declaring the gift of speaking in tongues is demonic is attributing the gift of God to Satan. **(Acts 2:1-4)** Which is blasphemy of the Holy Spirit. **(Mat. 12:31-32)**

‘If anyone comes to you and does not bring this doctrine, do not receive him into your house nor greet him; for he who greets him shares in his evil deeds.’ 2 John 1:10-11

Any believer transgressing the above doctrines of Christ no longer has God. To avoid sharing in their evil deeds, we aren't to fellowship with them. **(2 John 1:9-11)**

"Blessed is he who reads and those who hear the words of this prophecy, and keep those things which are written in it; for the time is near." Revelation 1:3

The Revelation of Jesus Christ was divinely given to John. **(Rev. 1:1-3)** The main focus is the Second Coming of Christ! **(Rev. 1:7)** Like His First Coming, there is a great responsibility for believers teaching the events, the timing, and the consequences of His Second Coming. **(Rev. 7:9-17; 10:1-7; 19:11-21; 21:9-10)**

"For I testify to everyone who hears the words of the prophecy of this book: If anyone adds to these things, God will add to him the plagues that are written in this book." Revelation 22:18

Jesus is warning believers hearing the words of The Revelation of Jesus Christ! **(Rev. 1:3)** No one is to deceive by adding to this prophecy. **(Rev. 22:18)** For those who do, they will suffer the last seven plagues, the wrath of the Lamb during the **Seven Bowls**. **(Rev. 6:16-17; 15:1; 16:1-21)**

'And I urge you also, true companion, help these women who labored with me in the gospel, with Clement also, and the rest of my fellow workers, whose names are in the Book of Life.'
Philippians 4:3

Only the names of believers are written in the Book of Life. **(Phil. 4:3)** Only the Lamb's wife will abide in the holy Jerusalem for eternity! **(Rev. 21:9-10, 27)** This final warning by Jesus is crystal clear! **(Rev. 22:19)** The Christians taking away from this prophecy, God promises to take away their part in the Book of Life and the holy city! Which means this is a salvation issue for believers taking away from the Second Coming of Christ! May the Spirit of God bear witness! **(Rev. 1:1-3)**

"And if anyone takes away from the words of the book of this prophecy, God shall take away his part from the Book of Life, from the holy city, and from the things which are written in this book."
Revelation 22:19

John was carried away in the Spirit to a high mountain. From there he saw the great city descending out of heaven from God! The Lamb and His wife are returning to a new earth inside the holy Jerusalem. **(Rev. 21:9-10)** Jesus is warning believers not to deceive by taking away the timing of this event! **(Rev. 22:19)** Sadly, most teachers are declaring this is not a salvation issue!

As one pastor once rebuked me:
"Paul, you're majoring in the minors. Believing how the Second Coming will turn out has nothing to do with our salvation! Just think of the hundreds of interpretations Christians are trusting in! (False)

Jesus is not saying you must understand the events of His Second Coming to be saved. **(Rev. 1:3)** Yet, His final warning is clearly protection for His saints. **(Rev. 22:19)** DECEIVING BY TAKING AWAY the timing of the Son of Man **(Rev. 7:9-17)**, the Holy One **(Rev. 10:1-7)**, the Word of God **(Rev. 19:11-21)**, and the Lamb of God **(Rev. 21:9-10)** is *unacceptable!* So why did our Lord feel the need to reveal the eternal punishment of believers who do? He is giving them an opportunity to repent. **(Rev. 3:3)** For those refusing, God will take away their part in the Book of Life and the holy Jerusalem! **(Rev. 20:15; 21:9-10)**

"As many as I love, I rebuke and chasten. Therefore be zealous and repent." Revelation 3:3

In his vision, John saw four visits by Jesus during His Second Coming! At this moment, very few believe this revelation by our Lord. In order to warn future overcomers, I would like to expose twelve deceptions denying these events depicted in The Revelation of Jesus Christ! **(Rev. 7:9-17; 10:1-7; 19:11-21; 21:9-10)**

Who is taking away from The Son of Man?
'I looked when He opened the sixth seal, and behold, there was a great earthquake; and the sun became black as sackcloth of hair, and the moon became like blood.' Revelation 6:12

A quote taking away the resurrection of believers
"There are no signs left to watch for. Jesus can come back at any moment." (False)

(1) The resurrection of dead and alive believers will initiate His Second Coming. **(Mark 13:24-27, 1 Thes. 4:15-17)** Every eye will see two signs during the future Great Tribulation. **(Rev. 7:9-17)** First, the sun, moon, and stars will refuse to shine. **(Mat. 24:29, Rev. 6:12-17)** This is the sign of the Day of The Lord. **(Isa. 13:9-11, Luke 21:25-27)** The second sign will look like lightning flashing from the east to the west. **(Mat. 24:27)** This is the sign of the Son of Man. **(Mat. 24:30)** A terrified world trapped in darkness will see the Son coming back in the glory of His Father. **(Rev. 1:7, Mat. 16:27)** At the great sound of a trumpet **(1 Cor. 15:52)**, angels will gather glorified believers out of the Great Tribulation before the throne of God in heaven. **(Rev. 7:9-17)** Later, His elect will be rewarded at the Judgment Seat of Christ. **(2 Cor. 5:10-11, Rev. 11:18)** Followed by their marriage to the Lamb of God. **(Rev. 19:7)**

'After these things I looked, and behold, a great multitude which no one could number, of all nations, tribes, peoples, and tongues, standing before the throne and before the Lamb, clothed with white robes with palm branches in their hands...These are the ones who come out of the great tribulation..." Revelation 7:9, 14

A quote taking away from the Great Tribulation

"The Great Tribulation is Gods wrath! Jesus will never allow His future bride to suffer the persecution by the Beast and his False Prophet." (False)

(2) John witnessed three time periods taking place inside the **70th Week** of Daniel. **(Dan. 9:24-27)** The Beginning of Sorrows, the Great Tribulation, and the beginning of the Day of The Lord. The rebellion by man during the Beginning of Sorrows will take place in the first half of this seven year prophecy. **(Mat. 24:4-8, Rev. 6:1-6)** The wrath of Satan during the Great Tribulation will begin the second half. **(Mat. 24:9-22, Rev. 6:7-11)** After the opening of the **Sixth Seal (Rev. 6:12-17)**, Jesus will end Satan's wrath against the saints. **(Rev. 12:12-17; 13:7)** In the twinkling of an eye, a great multitude of overcomers will come out of the Great Tribulation and stand before the Father and the Lamb. **(Rev. 7:9-17)** This same day the wicked left behind will suffer the wrath of the Lamb. **(Mat. 24:37-39, Rev. 6:16-17; 8:1-2)** The prophets call this the Day of The Lord. **(Isa. 13:9-11, Joel 2:30-31, 2 Thes. 2:1-4)**

‘Jesus said, “I am. And you will see the Son of Man sitting at the right hand of the Power, and coming with the clouds of heaven.” Mark 14:62

A quote taking away The Second Coming of Christ

“The Coming of the Son of Man is the same event as the appearing of the Word of God at the battle of Armageddon!” (False)

(3) In his vision in 96 A.D., John witnessed a great multitude of believers cloaked in darkness. **(Rev. 6:12-17)** They have come out of the Great Tribulation and are standing before the Father and the Lamb. **(Rev. 7:9-17)** The exact time Jesus taught the Son of Man will send forth angels to gather His elect to heaven. **(Mark 13:24-27)** Clearly, the apostle thought this will be the Second Coming of Christ! **(John 14:3, Luke 17:26-30)** Until he witnessed three more visits by Jesus. The physical return by the Holy One. **(Rev. 10:1-7)** The appearing by the Word of God. **(Rev. 19:11-21)** The arrival by the Lamb of God. **(Rev. 21:9-10)** Why did Jesus’ use *‘Coming’* only with the Son of Man? **(Mat. 24:37, Mark 13:26, Luke 21:27)** Our Lord did this because He wants us to understand when His Second Coming will begin. Coming means an arrival with an ensuing presence. **(Mark 14:62)** This is a revelation kept secret from the foundation of the world! **(1 Cor. 3:11)**

Who is taking away from The Most Holy?

'But in the days of the sounding of the seventh angel, when he is about to sound, the mystery of God would be finished, as He declared to His servants the prophets.' Revelation 10:7

A quote taking away from the return of Christ

"The Feasts of The Lord were fulfilled in the first century!" (False)

(1) After 490 years of domination by the Gentiles, the Most Holy will return to make an end to sins, make reconciliation for their iniquity, and bring in everlasting righteousness. **(Dan. 9:24)** One third of Israel will be eagerly waiting for the Christ to appear in the holy city, Jerusalem. **(Heb. 9:28, Zech. 13:8-9)** After the **70th Week** ends, the Christ will physically return a second time on the Day of Atonement. **(Rom. 11:25-27, Rev. 10:1-7)** Five days later, the Lamb of God will reap the final harvest of born again Jews. **(Rev. 14:14-16)** This ingathering will fulfill the Feast of Tabernacles. **(Rev. 14:1-4)** Yet, for centuries most pastors and teachers have taught these Feasts are past. Instead, they believe the first time the Son returns since He left to be with His Father (**Acts 1:11)** will be at the supper of the great God! **(Rev. 19:11-21)** Beware saints, this is not biblical. The Holy One will physically return after the sounding of the **Sixth Trumpet**. **(Rev. 10:1-7)** The Word of God won't appear until after the pouring out of the **Seventh Bowl**. **(Rev. 16:17-21)**

"But in the days of the sounding of the seventh angel, when he is about to sound, the mystery of God would be finished, as He declared to His servants the prophets." Revelation 10:7

A quote taking away the Mystery of God
"The resurrection of believers is the fulfillment of the mystery of God!" (False)

(2) The gathering of believers from heaven and earth by the Son of Man will take place during the **Feast of Trumpets. (Mark 13:24-27)** At the last trump, the sun, moon, and stars will lose their light, after the opening of the **Sixth Seal**. **(1 Cor. 15:50-52, Isa. 13:9-11, Rev. 6:12)** Every eye will see the Son coming in the glory of His Father! **(Rev. 1:7, Mat. 16:27, Mat. 24:29-31)** Which means the mystery of the resurrection will take place in the second half of the **70th Week**. **(Rev. 7:9-17)**

The gathering of born again Jews by the Most Holy will take place during the **Day of Atonement**. **(Dan. 9:24, Heb. 9:28, Rom. 11:25, Rev. 10:1-7)** The Christ will physically return a second time after the sounding of the **Sixth Trumpet**! **(Rev. 9:13-21; 10:1-7)** This mystery of God will take place after the fullness of the **70th Week** is completed. **(Rom. 11:25-27, Rev. 10:1-7)**

"Behold, I am coming quickly! Blessed is he who keeps the words of the prophecy of this book." Revelation 22:7

Jesus will fulfill the **Feast of Trumpets, the Day of Atonement** and the **Feast of Tabernacles** during His Second Coming. In his vision, John saw these holy days taking place at different times, for different reasons, each having a different result. **(Rev. 7:9-17; 10:17; 14:1-4)** Tragically, the many denying this truth are taking away from, The Revelation of Jesus Christ! **(Rev. 22:7, 19)**

'And they gathered them together to the place called in Hebrew, Armageddon. Then the seventh angel poured out his bowl into the air, and a loud voice came out of the temple of heaven, from the throne, saying, "It is done!" Revelation 16:16-17

A quote taking away the deliverance of Israel

"The Word will split the Mount of Olives at the supper of the great God." (False)

(3) The wrath from the Lamb will end after the **Seventh Bowl** is poured out on the wicked. **(Rev. 6:16-17; 15:1; 16:17)** After this, the Word and His armies of angels will come down to war against the Beast. **(Rev. 19:11-21)** Most Christians believe this is when our Lord will stand upon the Mount of Olives and split it in two. Yet, the reason for cutting this mountain in two is to create a place of safety from the last seven plagues. **(Rev. 15:1)** For in them the wrath of God is done. **(Rev. 16:17)** After an angel sounds the **Seventh Trumpet,** Jesus will split the Mount of Olives creating a mountain valley. The remnant from the Feast of Tabernacles will escape by fleeing through this valley to Azal. **(Zech. 14:3-5)** Anyone denying this protection of born again Jews is taking away from the Second Coming of Christ.

Who is taking away from The Word of God?

'Then the beast was captured, and with him the false prophet who worked signs in his presence, by which he deceived those who received the mark of the beast and those who worshiped his image. These two were cast alive into the lake of fire burning with brimstone.' Revelation 19:20

A quote taking away the timing of the Sheep from the Goats

"At the battle of Armageddon, Jesus will cast the goats' into everlasting fire prepared for the devil and his angels." (False)

(1) After His Coming, the Son of Man will sit on the throne of His glory. **(Mat. 25:31)** Believers from the nations will be gathered before Him. **(John 5:28-29)** This is the judgment of those practicing evil! **(John 3:20, Dan. 12:2, Mat. 25:46)** The wicked goats will be cursed into everlasting fire before the sheep are rewarded at the Judgment Seat of Christ. **(Mat. 25:41-46, 2 Cor. 5:10-11, Rom. 14:10)** Clearly, this separation will take place in heaven after the Coming of the Son of Man. **(Mat. 13:39-42; 25:31-46)** Not at the battle of Armageddon, nor at the Great White Throne Judgment. **(Rev. 16:14-16; 19:11-21; 20:11-15)**

'The devil, who deceived them, was cast into the lake of fire and brimstone where the beast and the false prophet are. And they will be tormented day and night forever and ever." Revelation 20:10

A quote taking away the Lake of Fire

"There is no such thing as a literal lake of fire for the wicked! The only punishment for rejecting His forgiveness is separation from God for eternity." (False)

(2) At this moment, there is a growing movement denying an everlasting lake of fire. I remember hearing a famous evangelist changing his theology after forty years. He now teaches the lake of fire is actually a burning thirst for God that can never be satisfied. I ask you, what is his motive behind such deception? At the great day of God Almighty, the Word of God will cast the Beast and the False Prophet into a literal lake of fire. **(Rev. 16:14-16; 19:20)** A thousand years later, Satan will join the two beasts in their suffering. **(Rev. 20:10)** They will be tormented day and night forever and ever. This evangelist is dismissing the second death of the wicked at the Great White Throne. **(Rev. 20:14)** To be clear, anyone denying the severity of this divine judgment is transgressing the doctrine of Christ. **(2 John 1:9-10)**

'And I saw the beast, the kings of the earth, and their armies gathered together to make war against Him who sat on the horse and against His army.' Revelation 19:19

A quote taking away from the Second Coming
"The resurrection of dead and alive believers will take place at the great day of God Almighty, Armageddon." (False)

(3) After the **Seventh Bowl,** the Word and His armies will strike the nations. **(Rev. 16:17-21; 19:11-21)** Jesus will begin by killing the followers of the Beast with a sword from His mouth. Birds will then eat their dead flesh at the supper of the great God. **(Rev. 19:17-18)** For centuries, the fivefold ministry has vainly taught this is the only time Jesus will return during His Second Coming. Yet, John saw Jesus fulfill the Feast of Trumpets **(Rev. 7:9-17)**, the Day of Atonement **(Rev. 10:1-7)**, and the Feast of Tabernacles **(Rev. 14:1-4)** before the Word of God appears at the supper of the great God. **(Rev. 19:11-21)** Which means His Second Coming is much more than a single visit! **(Rev. 22:7)**

Who is taking away from The Lamb of God?
'Blessed and holy is he who has part in the first resurrection. Over such the second death has no power, but they shall be priests of God and of Christ, and shall reign with Him a thousand years.' Revelation 20:6

<u>A quote taking away the timing of The Lamb of God</u>
"After a thousand years, the Lamb and His bride will descend to a new earth inside the Holy Jerusalem!" (False)

(1) Not all the events in John's vision will take place in chronological order. **(Rev. 1:1-3)** For example, most believe the Lamb and His bride will return after a thousand years. Yet, His Second Coming will end when the tabernacle of God is with men! **(Rev. 21:1-3)** This will happen the day the Lamb and His wife begin reigning from within the holy Jerusalem. **(Rev. 21:9-10)** Clearly, they will return to a new earth at the beginning of the millennium, not after! **(Rev. 20:6)** I've confronted many refusing to teach this truth. This shows how powerful the bondage is for those denying when the Lamb will complete His Second Coming.

'And out of the temple came the seven angels having the seven plagues, clothed in pure bright linen, and having their chests girded with golden bands.' Revelation 15:6

<u>A quote taking away the arrival by The Lamb of God</u>
"The bride clothed in fine linen, white and clean will return with the Word of God. The saints will be following Him on white horses. (False)

(2) For centuries, most bible teachers have taught the armies returning with the Word of God are His resurrected saints. **(Rev. 19:14)** The truth is the saints will be rewarded according to their works at the Judgment Seat of Christ in heaven. **(Mat. 16:27, Rev. 11:18)** Followed by their marriage to the Lamb of God. **(Rev. 19:7)** This ceremony will take place before the Word casts the Beast and False Prophet into the lake of fire. **(Rev. 19:11-21)** Clearly, the bride will return from heaven to earth one time. Yet, John didn't see the bride at the supper of the great God. **(Rev. 19:17)** Instead, the apostle later saw the Lamb and His bride arriving on a new earth inside the Holy Jerusalem. **(Dan. 12:12, Rev. 20:6; 21:9-10)** Which means the armies riding on white horses are not His saints! **(Rev. 19:14)** His armies, clothed in pure bright linen, are actually angels. **(Rev. 15:6)**

"Behold, I am coming as a thief. Blessed is he who watches, and keeps his garments, lest he walk naked and they see his shame." Revelation 16:15

A quote taking away the events of His Second Coming!

"Jesus is coming back one more time." (False)

(3) For centuries, most have taught the Second Coming is a single event.

They were unable to see the events Jesus will fulfill!

The Son of Man **after the 6th Seal**. **(Rev. 7:9-17)**

The Most Holy **after the 6th Trumpet. (Rev. 10:1-7)**

The Word of God **after the 7th Bowl. (Rev. 19:11-21)**

The Lamb of God **reigning** over a new earth. **(Rev. 21:9-10)**

Clearly, these are four different events. Each one having a different result. Any believer denying this revelation is taking away the events, timing and consequences of the Second Coming of Christ. **(Rev. 22:19)**

'Then He said to them, "Thus it is written, and thus it was necessary for the Christ to suffer and to rise from the dead the third day, and that repentance and remission of sins should be preached in His name to all nations, beginning at Jerusalem. And you are witnesses of these things. Behold, I send the Promise of My Father upon you; but tarry in the city of Jerusalem until you are endued with power from on high." Luke 24:46-49

Before being carried up into heaven, it was necessary for the Christ to suffer and die on the cross. **(Luke 24:46-49)** This was the fulfillment of the Feast of Passover! **(Lev. 23:5)** To be buried during the Feast of Unleavened Bread! **(Lev. 23:6-8)** To rise from the dead during the Feast of First Fruits! **(Lev. 23:10-14)** This is the gospel of our Lord Jesus Christ! **(1 Cor. 15:1-4)** Beginning in Jerusalem, the repentance and remission of sins in His name will be preached to all nations. His apostles were witnesses of these things. The night of His resurrection, Jesus breathed on them and they received the indwelling of the Holy Spirit. **(John 20:22)** Forty days later, Jesus exhorted them to wait for The Promise of The Father. **(Acts 1:4-5)** They were to tarry in Jerusalem until being endued with power from on high! Ten days later, during the

Feast of Weeks, they were baptized with the Holy Spirit. On the Day of Pentecost, they spoke in tongues as the Spirit gave them utterance! **(Acts 2:1-4)**

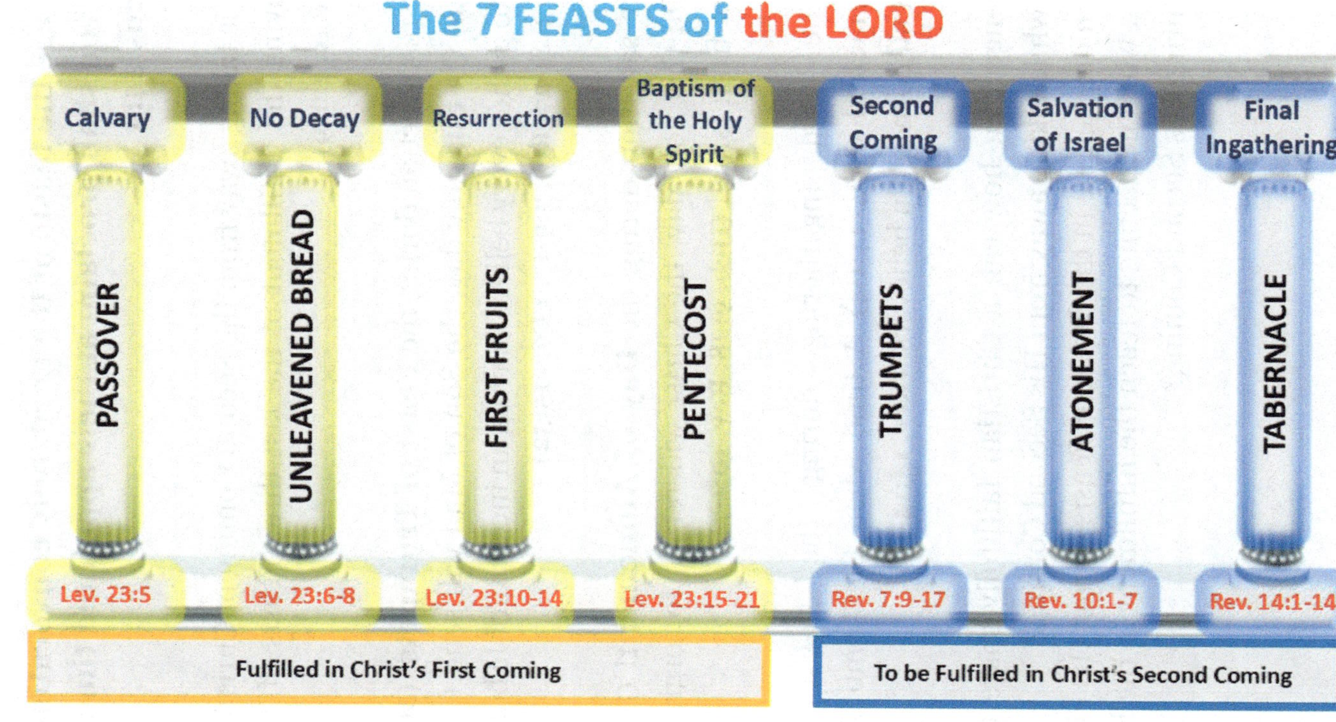
The 7 FEASTS of the LORD
Calvary
No Decay
Resurrection
Baptism of the Holy Spirit
Second Coming
Salvation of Israel
Final Ingathering
PASSOVER
UNLEAVENED BREAD
FIRST FRUITS
PENTECOST
TRUMPETS
ATONEMENT
TABERNACLE
Lev. 23:5
Lev. 23:6-8
Lev. 23:10-14
Lev. 23:15-21
Rev. 7:9-17
Rev. 10:1-7
Rev. 14:1-14
Fulfilled in Christ's First Coming
To be Fulfilled in Christ's Second Coming

'These are the feasts of the Lord, holy convocations which you shall proclaim at their appointed times.' Leviticus 24:4

So who is taking away from the Second Coming of Christ? All denying the fulfillment of the last three Feasts of The Lord! **(Rev. 22:19)**

(1) The resurrection during the **Feast of Trumpets**! **(Mat. 24:29-36)** On this holy day, the Son of Man will send forth angels to gather every believer having an incorruptible body! **(Mark 13:24-27, Rev. 7:9-17, 1 Cor. 15:52)**

(2) The salvation during the **Day of Atonement**! **(Dan. 9:24)** On this holy day, the Christ will return to forgive a remnant from Israel! **(Heb. 9:28, Rev. 10:1-7)**

(3) The final ingathering during the **Feast of Tabernacles**! **(Rev. 14:1-4)** A time when the Lamb will harvest all born again believers! **(Rev. 14:14-16)**

I challenge you; how can a Christian faithfully share the gospel while taking away from His Second Coming?
How can one believe in the first four Feasts during His First Coming, while neglecting to teach the fulfillment of the last three during His Second Coming?

Why does this matter to our Jesus?
The many denying these future Feasts are:
Taking away the Blessed Hope from believers!
Taking away the offer of salvation for the children of Israel!
Taking away the final harvest from the wrath to come!

"Behold, I am coming quickly! Blessed is he who keeps the words of the prophecy of this book." Revelation 22:7

In this late hour, may Jesus open our understanding. That we might comprehend the events, timing, and consequences of His Second Coming. Amen!

"If you take away from His Second Coming, His First Coming won't save you."
Paul Bortolazzo

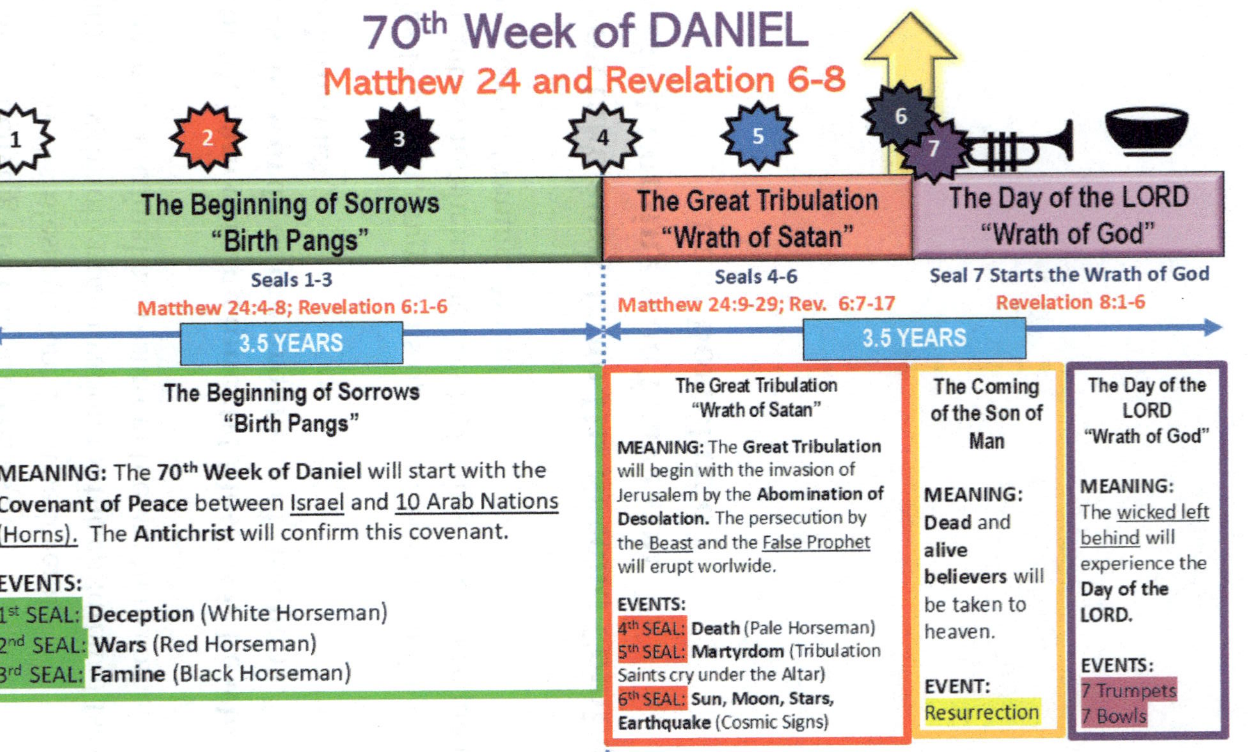
70th Week of DANIEL
Matthew 24 and Revelation 6-8
1
2
3
4
5
6
7
The Beginning of Sorrows
"Birth Pangs"
The Great Tribulation
"Wrath of Satan"
The Day of the LORD
"Wrath of God"
Seals 1-3
Matthew 24:4-8; Revelation 6:1-6
Seals 4-6
Matthew 24:9-29; Rev. 6:7-17
Seal 7 Starts the Wrath of God
Revelation 8:1-6
3.5 YEARS
3.5 YEARS
The Beginning of Sorrows
"Birth Pangs"
MEANING: The 70th Week of Daniel will start with the Covenant of Peace between Israel and 10 Arab Nations (Horns). The Antichrist will confirm this covenant.
EVENTS:
1st SEAL: Deception (White Horseman)
2nd SEAL: Wars (Red Horseman)
3rd SEAL: Famine (Black Horseman)
The Great Tribulation
"Wrath of Satan"
MEANING: The Great Tribulation will begin with the invasion of Jerusalem by the Abomination of Desolation. The persecution by the Beast and the False Prophet will erupt worlwide.
EVENTS:
4th SEAL: Death (Pale Horseman)
5th SEAL: Martyrdom (Tribulation Saints cry under the Altar)
6th SEAL: Sun, Moon, Stars, Earthquake (Cosmic Signs)
The Coming of the Son of Man
MEANING: Dead and alive believers will be taken to heaven.
EVENT: Resurrection
The Day of the LORD
"Wrath of God"
MEANING: The wicked left behind will experience the Day of the LORD.
EVENTS:
7 Trumpets
7 Bowls

The Glossary

Abomination of Desolation

The Antichrist has several names. Daniel calls him, the Little Horn. Jesus calls him, the Abomination of Desolation. Paul calls him, the Man of Sin. John calls him the Beast. The world will be watching when this evil leader confirms a peace covenant between Israel and the leaders from ten Arab nations (horns). Three and a half years later, he will reveal his true identity. He will invade an unsuspecting Jerusalem with the armies from ten nations. After exalting himself in the temple of God, the Man of Sin will be called the abomination that causes desolation.

Apocalypse

Apocalypse is an 'unveiling.' The unveiling of, The Revelation of Jesus Christ, will be the events taking place before, during and after His Second Coming. Any believer adding or taking away from this prophecy, God will take away their part in the Book of Life and thc holy Jerusalem.

Apostasy

According to the apostle Paul, apostasy is a departure from the faith. Christians will be hated by all nations during the days of the Great Tribulation. Under intense persecution by the False Prophet, the love for Christ will grow cold. At that time, rather than enduring until the harvest, many will fall away from their faith by worshiping the Beast, his image and receiving his mark.

Armageddon

The second half of the 70th Week of Daniel will last 1260 days. Thirty days later (1290 days), the Word and His armies of angels will appear at the great day of God Almighty, Armageddon. The Beast and his armies will suffer the fierceness of the wrath of Almighty God. Jesus will begin by casting the Beast and the False Prophet into the lake of fire. Before killing their followers at the supper of the great God.

Atonement, Day of

The Day of Atonement was instituted by God. Each year, on this holy day, the sins committed by the Jewish people were forgiven by God. This future Feast of the Lord, Yom Kippur, will be fulfilled by the Most Holy. After the 490-year prophecy by Daniel is over, the Christ will physically return a second time to save all believing in Him. This is the fulfillment of the Mystery of God by Jesus.

Azal

After the sounding of the Seventh Trumpet, Jesus will create a shield of protection against the last seven plagues, the Seven Bowls! Standing on the Mount of Olives, He will split it in two. The believers at the Feast of Tabernacles will flee through this mountain valley to Azal. Once this surviving remnant safely reaches this refuge, the Lamb of God will destroy the kingdom of the Beast.

Beast, the First

Satan will give his power over the nations to the Beast for the entire second half of the 70th Week (1260 days). This world leader, the Abomination of Desolation, will begin by invading an unsuspecting Jerusalem. The Beast will then order all dwelling on the earth to worship him. Anyone not having his mark on their forehead or right hand won't be able to buy or sell anything. This mark, 666, is a sign of allegiance. All receiving it will suffer the wrath of God. They will eventually be tormented in the presence of the Lamb. Once the 70th Week is completed, the Beast will kill the Two Witnesses. Thirty days later, the Word of God will cast this deceiver into the lake of fire at the supper of the great God.

Beast, the Second

The first Beast is also called the Man of Sin. He will be joined by a second beast. The False Prophet will exercise all the authority of the first Beast while in his presence. This second beast will deceive the world by performing great signs. During the Great Tribulation, he will have the power to kill anyone (man, woman or child) refusing to worship the Beast.

Beginning of Sorrows

The deception by false teachers, wars, famines, earthquakes, and pestilences will take place in the first half of the future 70th Week of Daniel. Jesus calls these events the Beginning of Sorrows. The riders of the white, red, and black horses will use this suffering to bring the world to its knees in submission. The Great Tribulation will begin the second half of this seven year covenant. The same day the rider of the pale horse comes down to earth. During the Great Tribulation, Death will have the power to kill one fourth of the world through the two beasts.

Blessed Hope

Our Blessed Hope has promised to come back for His elect. The apostle Paul calls it, the glorious appearing of our great God and Savior Jesus Christ. At the last trumpet, the Son of Man will deliver a great multitude of believers out of the Great Tribulation. The empowering of the saints to get the victory over the Beast does not take away our Blessed Hope; it enhances it.

Bowl Judgments

John saw the angels having the last seven plagues. All having the mark of the Beast will suffer the misery from these seven bowl judgments. This horrific wrath will be poured out in the thirty-day period following the completion of the 70th Week. (1260/1290 days) The Day of The Lord will erupt with fire after the opening of the Seventh Seal. It will end after the pouring out of the Seventh Bowl. A time when great hailstones will fall on all blaspheming God.

Bride, of Christ

Old and New Testament believers will receive incorruptible bodies at the Coming of the Son of Man. After their resurrection unto eternal life, they will stand before the Judgment Seat of Christ. Each saint will be rewarded according to their works. Later they will be married to the Lamb of God. On the first day of their 1,000 year reign, the Lamb and His bride will arrive on a new earth inside the holy Jerusalem.

Christ, First Coming

Many witnessed the First Coming of Christ. It began with His virgin birth in a manger. The Messiah was twelve when He shared with teachers. The Lamb of God was baptized in water by John. The Son of Man healed the sick, cast out demons, and preached the gospel. His First Coming ended after He died on a cross, rose from the dead and ascended to His Father. As a result, the Son of God reversed the eternal consequences of sin and death for mankind. His sinless sacrifice provides eternal life for all believing in Him as their Lord and Savior.

Christ, Second Coming

The Second Coming of Christ is more than a single event. It has a beginning and an ending. Jesus has promised to come back for His bride. It will begin with the resurrection at the Coming of The Son of Man. At the last trump, angels will gather believers from heaven and earth. Later, the Most Holy will physically return for the salvation of Israel. At

Armageddon, the Word will cast the Beast and the False Prophet into the lake of fire. His Second Coming will end when the Lamb of God and His wife arrive on a new earth to rule for a thousand years.

Church

To join the church, the body of Christ, one must be born again by the Spirit of God. All abiding in the doctrine of Christ have the Father, the Son, and the Holy Spirit. Believers transgressing the doctrine of Christ no longer have God.

Covenant, with Death

The Beast (Antichrist) will confirm a seven-year covenant of peace between Israel and the leaders from ten Arab horns (nations). The prophet Isaiah calls this a covenant with death. Most Jews will believe this pact will prevent further attacks from their enemies. That is until they see the Abomination of Desolation and his armies surrounding Jerusalem. This is the beginning of Jacobs Trouble. Over two thirds from Israel will be cut off and die during the second half of the 70th Week.

Day of The Lord

The Day of The Lord is the most prophesied event in the Bible! After the opening of the Seventh Seal, the wrath of the Lamb will punish the world for its evil. Jesus will begin by destroying sinners. The Day of The Lord is comprised of two time periods. The first is angels sounding seven trumpets.

The second will be angels pouring out seven bowls. Gods' final wrath will end after the Seventh Bowl. Culminating at the great day of God Almighty, Armageddon.

Dead in Christ

At the Coming of The Lord, Jesus will bring with Him believers from heaven. At the last trump, the dead in Christ will be changed, receiving incorruptible bodies. In the twinkling of an eye, alive believers will join them. They will all be caught up before the Judgment Seat of Christ in heaven. After being rewarded according to their works, they will be married to the Lamb of God.

Diaspora, of Israel

The diaspora of Israel took place after their rejection of their Messiah. In 70 A.D., Roman armies invaded Jerusalem and destroyed their temple. In 132 A.D., the remaining Jews were expelled from Jerusalem. They were scattered all over the world. This lasted until Israel became a nation in 1948! Millions of Jews have returned to their homeland in unbelief. During His Second Coming, the Christ will return on the Day of Atonement. The Most Holy will spiritually and physically save a remnant from the house of Israel.

Feasts of The Lord

During His First Coming, our Messiah fulfilled the first four Feasts of The Lord. The Feast of Passover represents His shedding of blood on the cross for the sins of the world. The Feast of Unleavened Bread represents the time His body did not decay in the grave. The Feast of First Fruits represents His resurrection from the dead on the third day. The Feast of Weeks (Pentecost) represents the day believers received the Promise of the Father. The baptism in the Holy Spirit with the initial evidence of speaking in tongues.

Jesus will fulfill the last three Feasts during His Second Coming. During the Feast of Trumpets, the Son of Man will deliver the righteous before pouring out His wrath on the wicked obeying the Beast. During the Day of Atonement, the Holy One will spiritually save a remnant from Israel. During the Feast of Tabernacles, the Lamb of God will harvest all born-again believers before destroying the wicked.

Gentiles, Time of The

This is the end time prophecy Gabriel gave Daniel. Due to their refusal to repent of their sins, God has decreed a chastisement of the Jewish people. The Gentiles will dominate Israel for seventy weeks. One week represents seven years (7x70=490 years). This punishment began with the captivity of Jews in Babylon. The fullness of the Gentiles will end when the 70th Week is completed. The fulfillment of this prophecy is the salvation of Israel. How so? The Christ will physically return a second time and forgive all believing in Him.

Great Tribulation

In the middle of the 70th Week, Michael the restrainer, will cast the accuser of the brethren out of heaven for the final time. Satan will come down to earth having great wrath. He will begin by giving the Beast His power over the nations. This same day, the Beast will command the world to worship his image and receive his mark. This edict will initiate the days of the Great Tribulation. The future redemption of alive believers will cut short this satanic persecution. On the same day, the wrath of the Lamb will begin destroying sinners left behind.

Great White Throne

The Lamb of God and His wife will rule over a new earth from within a new heaven. After their thousand-year reign is over, the wicked dead will be resurrected out of Hades. They will stand before the Great White Throne. Jesus will judge them before casting them into the lake of fire. This torment is the second death.

Harvest, Wheat and Tares

At the harvest, the Son of Man will send forth His angels. These reapers will gather the wheat with the tares. The wheat are the faithful sons of the kingdom. The tares practicing lawlessness are now the sons of the wicked one. From the throne of His glory in heaven, Jesus will cast these apostates into everlasting fire. Then the righteous will shine forth in the kingdom of their Father.

Horn, Little

Before the 70th Week begins, a world leader will emerge in the Middle East. The Little Horn will speak pompous words against the Most High. This deceiver, also called the Beast, will gain the support of ten Arab nations surrounding Israel. He will then confirm a covenant of peace between Jews and Muslims. This seven-year covenant is the 70th Week of Daniel. Never called the Tribulation Period.

Horsemen, Four

John saw the events of the Beginning of Sorrows. The riders of the white, red, and black horses will initiate the events from the first three seals of the heavenly scroll. The deception by false teachers, wars, famines, earthquakes, and pestilences will take place in the first half of the 70th Week. The Great Tribulation will begin the day the Lamb opens the Fourth Seal. The rider of the pale horse, Death, will come down having the power to kill one fourth of mankind.

Imminence

Imminence means 'at any moment.' Today, most pastors are vainly teaching there are no events left to be fulfilled before the Coming of our Lord. This is why most are expecting to be caught up at any moment. Yet, the only time the Son can return at any moment is after the constellations lose their light, the sign of the Day of the Lord! During the Feast of Trumpets, the resurrection of believers by the Son of Man will take place after the opening of the Sixth Seal.

Israel, the Salvation of

During the Great Tribulation, an unsaved remnant from Israel will survive the persecution by the False Prophet. Only to face a divine purification during the Day of The Lord. This spiritual cleansing by God will result in their salvation. The Most Holy will fulfill the Mystery of God on the Day of Atonement. Jesus will say this is my people. This saved remnant will say, *'The LORD is my God.'*

Jacobs Trouble, Time of

Daniels description of Jacobs Trouble is synonymous with Jesus' description of the Great Tribulation. The church and unsaved Israel will experience this time of trouble during the 70th Week of Daniel. Satan's wrath will begin the day the Fourth Seal opens. It will be amputated after the opening of the Sixth Seal. The same day the wrath of the Lamb is poured out on the wicked left behind.

Jerusalem, the Invasion of

In the first half of the 70th Week prophecy, the nations will suffer the horror of wars while Israel is being protected. The second half will begin with the invasion of Jerusalem by the armies of the Beast. While sitting in the rebuilt temple, the Man of Sin will speak blasphemy against God, His tabernacle, and those dwelling in heaven. After defiling the holy place, he will be called the abomination that causes desolation. The Beast will then demand the world to worship him and take his mark. This is the beginning of the Great Tribulation.

Judgment Seat of Christ

After the resurrection of believers, the Son will sit on the throne of His glory in heaven. From His Bema Seat, the Judgment Seat of Christ, every saint will give an account of themselves. All works built upon the foundation of Jesus Christ will be rewarded. The works done in the flesh will burn up. Some will be called great in the kingdom, while others will be called least for eternity!

Kingdom of Israel

The day after the 70th Week ends, the Christ will physically return a second time to restore the Kingdom of Israel. This restoration will begin with the salvation of Israel on The Day of Atonement. Five days later, the final harvest of born-again Jews will celebrate the Feast of Tabernacles. This restoration will be completed after the Lamb and His bride arrive on a new earth to rule for a thousand years.

Last Day

The last day will initiate the Day of The Lord. The same day believers are caught up out of the Great Tribulation by angels, the wrath of the Lamb will be poured out upon the wicked left behind. Like in the days of Noah and Lot, the day the righteous are delivered, God will begin destroying the unrighteous.

Marriage Supper of The Lamb

The Lamb will marry His bride before the great day of God Almighty. Forty-five days after the battle of Armageddon

(1290-1335 days), the Lamb and His wife will descend to a new earth inside a new heaven. And who will partake in the marriage supper during the thousand year reign of Christ? It will be the surviving believers on earth and the wife of the Lamb abiding within the New Jerusalem.

Martyrs, Fifth Seal

The Great Tribulation will begin the second half of the 70th Week. The rider of the pale horse, Death, will come down to earth. Everyone refusing to obey the Beast will be persecuted. The faithful believers caught by the False Prophet will be killed. After the opening of the Fifth Seal, John saw these martyrs in heaven! During the Great Tribulation, they refused to worship the Beast, his image, or receive his mark! The result, they will receive a special reward for being faithful unto death. They will be resurrected on the first day of Christ's reign over a new earth!

Most Holy

God committed the Jewish people to disobedience so the Gentiles could be saved. The day after the 70th Week is completed, the Most Holy will physically return a second time on the Day of Atonement. The Christ will spiritually and physically save a surviving one third from Israel believing in Him.

Millennium

Millennium means 'thousand.' The Lamb of God and His wife will rule for a thousand years over a new earth. The holy city from above, the New Jerusalem, will join physical Jerusalem on earth. They will rule for eternity from both.

Mystery, of God

After the 70th Week is over, the Most Holy will fulfill the mystery of God. The Christ will physically return a second time in the clouds for the salvation of Israel. Five days later, the Lamb will complete the Feast of Tabernacles by the final harvest of born-again Jews.

Noah, Days of

The Son of Man will be like the days of Noah. The same day God closed the door to the ark, forty days of rain overwhelmed the wicked. Noah and his family escaped the wrath of God. Likewise, the same day angels gather alive believers to heaven, the wrath of the Lamb will begin destroying the wicked left behind.

Olivet Discourse

Just days before His death, Jesus met with His disciples atop the Mount of Olives. They wanted to know the sign of His Coming. Jesus began by sharing the future events that will warn believers His Coming is near. The events of the Beginning of Sorrows followed by the events of the Great Tribulation. After the constellations lose their light, every believer will be looking up for their redemption. This is the sign of the Day of The Lord, the opening of the Sixth Seal. Cloaked in darkness, every overcomer will see the Son coming back in the glory of His Father. In the twinkling of an eye, a great multitude of overcomers will be caught up before the throne of God. This same day, the wrath of the Lamb will begin punishing the world for its evil. The prophets call it, the Day of The Lord.

Overcomers

During the Great Tribulation, a great multitude from every nation will overcome the Beast by the blood of the Lamb and the word of their testimony. Jesus promises not to blot them out of the Book of Life. Instead, the Son will confess their names before His Father! Tragically, the saints overcome by the Beast will drink the wine of the wrath of God. They'll be tormented with fire in the presence of the Lamb.

Parables

Throughout His ministry, Jesus used parables to teach the mysteries of the kingdom. A parable is an earthly story with a heavenly meaning. During His Olivet Discourse our Lord used four parables describing the Coming of The Son of Man. Throughout history, believers' having dull hearts have not understood the meaning of the fig tree, the unfaithful servant, the ten virgins and the talents. Nor His metaphor of the sheep and the goats. Jesus is actually teaching the consequences faithful and unfaithful believers will receive after His Coming!

Periods, 1,260, 1,290, 1,335 days

The second half of the 70th Week will last 1,260 days. Thirty days later (1,290), the Word of God will appear at the supper of the great God. Jesus will begin by casting the two beasts into the lake of fire. Before killing their followers. Forty-five days later (1,335), the Lamb and His bride will descend to a new earth.

Persecution

The persecution during the Great Tribulation is Satan's wrath against those having the testimony of Jesus. Many of the faithful will be killed by the False Prophet. At the same time, there will be saints overcome by the Beast. These apostates will hate and betray the overcomers enduring till the harvest.

Reapers

In the parable of the wheat and tares, the Son of Man will send forth angels to reap a harvest. The wheat represents the faithful believers overcoming the Beast during the days of the Great Tribulation. The tares are the unfaithful believers practicing lawlessness. This harvest is twofold. The righteous will be resurrected unto eternal life. While the unrighteous will be cast into everlasting fire.

Redemption

Once Christians begin to suffer persecution during the Great Tribulation, they will know the Coming of The Son of Man is drawing near. After the constellations lose their light, a great multitude of overcomers will be looking up for their redemption. Their deliverance by angels can take place at any moment!

Remnant, Jewish

The very day Satan is cast down; the Woman will flee into the wilderness to a place prepared by God. This Jewish remnant will be protected for the entire second half of the 70th Week. Which means they will survive Satan's wrath during the Great Tribulation and God's wrath during the Day of The Lord. After the 70th Week is completed, the Most Holy will save one third of Israel. They'll be praising the Lamb on the first day of His 1,000 year reign over a new earth.

Restrainer, Michael

Michael is the great prince standing watch over the children of Israel. In the first half of the 70th Week, this archangel will be restraining the Beast, the mystery of lawlessness, from attacking the Jewish people. The second half will begin the day Michael casts the accuser of the brethren out of heaven for the final time. Satan will come down to earth having great wrath. With Michael's restraint removed, the Beast will have the freedom to persecute unsaved Israel and all having the testimony of Jesus Christ.

Saints, the Elect

Today, there is no Jew or Gentile within the body of Christ. Old Testament believers looked forward to the future coming of the Messiah. Those living after the cross, also believe in the Son of the Living God. To be a saint one must be born again by the Spirit. All believing in Jesus as their Lord and Savior will become His future bride.

Scroll, Large

In his vision, John saw the Father holding a large scroll in His right hand. The outside of the scroll is sealed with seven seals. The Lamb of God will open the first three seals in the first half of the 70th Week! He will open the last four seals in the second half of this seven year covenant.

Seals, Seven

After the opening of the **First Seal**, a rider on a white horse will come down to earth. His mission is to conquer many believers through false teachers. This same day, the Beast will confirm a false peace between Jews and Muslims. These two events will initiate the first half of the 70th Week of Daniel.

After the opening of the **Second Seal**, a rider on a red horse will emerge. He will have the power to take peace from the earth. He will do this by creating wars and rumors of wars. In the first half of the 70th Week many will kill one another.

After the opening of the **Third Seal**, a rider on a black horse will appear. He is holding a pair of scales. He will create famines, earthquakes, and pestilences on the earth. The events from the first three seals Jesus calls the Beginning of Sorrows. The suffering from these events will cease in the middle of the 70th Week.

After the opening of the **Fourth Seal**, a rider on a pale horse will go forth. He is called Death. Hades is following him. This will happen on the first day of the second half of the 70th Week. They will have the power to kill over one fourth of the earth through the Beast and the False Prophet.

After the opening of the **Fifth Seal**, John saw souls under the altar in heaven. They will be killed by the False Prophet for their testimony of Jesus during the Great Tribulation! These overcomers will ask the Lord to avenge their blood. They were told to rest until the number of their fellow martyrs is completed.

After the opening of the **Sixth Seal**, the entire earth will be cloaked in darkness. This is called the sign of the Day of The Lord. This same day, every eye will see the sign of the Son of Man. It will look like lightening flashing to the east to the west. Everyone will see the Son coming back in the glory of His Father! In the twinkling of an eye, all believers will receive incorruptible bodies. Angels will then take them before the throne of His glory, the Judgment Seat of Christ!

After the opening of the **Seventh Seal**, there will be silence in heaven. After a half an hour, an angel will cast a censor filled with fire to earth. The Day of The Lord, the destruction of sinners by the wrath of the Lamb, is underway!

Seventieth Week of Daniel

The last seven years of Israel's blindness is called the 70th Week of Daniel. It will begin when the Beast confirms a covenant of peace between Israel and ten Arab nations (horns). In the middle of the 70th Week, the Abomination of Desolation and his armies will surround an unsuspecting Jerusalem. The Man of Sin (Beast) will defile the temple of God after demanding the world worship him. For all refusing, they will face the greatest persecution in history! During the Feast of Trumpets, the Son of Man will deliver a great multitude of overcomers out of the Great Tribulation. At the end of the 70th Week, the Most Holy will return on the Day of Atonement to fulfill the mystery of God. Thirty days later, the Word of God and His armies will cast the two beasts into the lake of fire. Forty-five days later, the Lamb of God and His bride will reign over a new earth.

Seventh Trumpet

After the sounding of the Sixth Trumpet, the Most Holy will physically come back a second time. He will fulfill the mystery of God on the Day of Atonement. The Christ will forgive the sins of a surviving remnant hiding in the wilderness. Five days later, Jesus will complete the final harvest of believers to Jerusalem. From atop Mount Zion, the Lamb will celebrate the Feast of Tabernacles with the first fruits saved from Israel, the 144,000. Loud voices in heaven will announce the next event. At the sounding of the Seventh Trumpet, the Devil will be stripped of his power. The kingdoms of this world will become the kingdoms of our

Lord and of His Christ. The above events will take place in the thirty-day period after the 70th Week is completed.

Sheep and Goats

There will be a resurrection of dead and alive believers at the Coming of The Son of Man. At this time, angels will gather faithful and unfaithful believers before the throne of His glory. Before rewarding His sheep at the Judgment Seat of Christ, Jesus will cast the goats practicing evil into a furnace of fire. An everlasting fire originally prepared for the Devil and his angels.

Sign, The Day of the Lord

The constellations losing their light is the sign of the Day of The Lord. This blackout will take place after the Lamb opens the Sixth Seal. Amidst this darkness, every eye will see the Son coming back in the glory of His Father. After the resurrection of believers, the Lamb will open the Seventh Seal. There will be a half an hour of silence in heaven, before the sinners left behind suffer the wrath of the Lamb. The prophets call this wrath, the Day of The Lord.

Sign, The Son of Man

While on the Mount of Olives, Jesus taught the sign of The Son of Man. After the heavens lose their light, His Coming will look like lightening flashing from the east to the west. Every eye will see the Son coming back in the glory of His Father. At any moment, angels will gather a great multitude of overcomers out of the Great Tribulation. They will stand before the Judgment Seat of Christ in heaven.

Tabernacles, Feast of

On the Day of Atonement, the Most Holy will physically return to fulfill the Mystery of God, the salvation of Israel. Five days later, the Lamb will complete the final harvest of born again believers. During the Feast of Tabernacles, they will all declare, *"The LORD is my God."*

Temple, Seventieth Week

Titus and his Roman armies invaded Jerusalem in 70 A.D. While destroying their temple they killed many Jews. Jesus is warning us of another invasion of the holy place. In the middle of the 70th Week, the Man of Sin (Beast) will defile the rebuilt temple in Jerusalem by exalting himself above God! After placing an image of himself inside the holy place, the Beast (Antichrist) will be called the Abomination of Desolation! This is an expression for worshiping an idol in the place of God.

Trumpets, Feast of

The Feast of Trumpets is called, 'the day of the blowing of the shofar.' The future bride of Christ will be caught up to heaven at the last trump. No one will know the day or hour, the sun, moon, and stars will lose their light during this holy Feast. Amidst this darkness, every eye will see the Son coming back in the glory of His Father. This resurrection of believers will initiate His Second Coming.

Trumpet, Last

Only the Son of Man will fulfill the Feast of Trumpets. At the last trump, believers from heaven and earth will be changed. After receiving incorruptible bodies, holy angels will gather them before the throne of God in heaven.

Witnesses, The Two

The day the Abomination of Desolation and his armies invade Israel; the Two Witnesses will be watching. We aren't told their names. God will give them the power to prophesy the entire second half of the 70th Week. If any of their enemies try to harm them, they will be killed by fire proceeding from their mouths. The day after the 70th Week ends, the Beast will kill them. This same day, Jesus will physically return on the Day of Atonement for the salvation of Israel.

Woman, The

The Woman represents a remnant of Jews hiding in the wilderness during the second half of the 70th Week. The twelve stars on her head, represent 144,000 men from the twelve tribes of Israel. After the 70th Week ends, Jesus will gather them from the wilderness. Five days later, the Lamb and His first fruits saved will stand atop Mount Zion during the Feast of Tabernacles.

Wrath of The Lamb

The wrath of the Lamb will begin destroying sinners after the constellations lose their light, the sign of the Day of The

Lord. Trapped in darkness, the world will see Jesus coming back in the glory of His Father! At any moment, angels will gather a great multitude of overcomers out of the Great Tribulation. On the same day, the Lamb will open the Seventh Seal. After thirty minutes of silence in heaven, His wrath will punish the world for its evil. The Day of the Lord will end after the last seven plagues are poured out on the followers of the Beast.

Wrath, Satan's

The second half of the 70th Week will begin the day Michael casts Satan down to earth. Death, the rider of the pale horse, will arrive on the same day having the power to kill a fourth of mankind. Immediately, the armies of the Beast will surround an unwalled Jerusalem. This surprise attack will initiate Satan's great wrath during the Great Tribulation. The massive killing by the False Prophet will be cut short after the resurrection of overcomers by the Son of Man.

Made in the USA
Monee, IL
31 August 2025

23506708R00134